I0424851

Beyond the Border

Envisioning the Adversary's Tactics

by

Francisco "Frankie" Aviles

Table of Contents

Introduction:
Crafting the Adversary's Mindset

To understand the battlefield of ideas that shapes the nation, one must embark on a journey into the psyche of those who stand in opposition. The art of weaving through the intricacies of the adversary's thought patterns is not merely an academic pursuit; it is an essential survival skill in the treacherous terrain of political discourse. This introduction lays the foundation for a deep dive into the mental constructs that drive our nation's most pressing debates and decisions.

The concept of the adversary's mindset is not about demonization nor oversimplification of complex characters. It's about gaining a profound insight into why our opponents think the way they do, what motivates them, and how they articulate their vision for the future of our society. By understanding these dimensions, we position ourselves not only to anticipate their moves but also to effectively engage in the push and pull that defines our democratic process.

Imagine for a moment, walking a mile in the shoes of those you disagree with—not to adopt their creed, but to understand their reasoning. To empathically map out their intellectual terrain, their rationalizations, emotions, and moral compass. By doing so, we begin to see the world through their lens and consequently uncover the roots of conflict and the seeds of resolution.

Chapter 1 takes us through the labyrinth of 'Decoding the Adversary's Thinking,' a meticulous examination of their ideological framework. However, before we delve into the nuances of opposing thought processes, we must first set the stage. It's essential not to entangle ourselves in the weeds of the topics that follow but to understand the broader picture at play.

Strategic foresight is a cornerstone of what we will explore, anticipating not just the likely, but also the improbable. Chapter 2 explores this theme, but in this introduction, we highlight the importance of 'Preparing for the Unseen,' a precept that elevates strategy from reactionary to visionary.

The battlegrounds are many, and on each, the mindset of the adversary differs. The chapters to come will explore the nuances of immigration, partisanship, and the narrative battles that encompass the socialist threat, faith in politics, the right to bear arms, economic policy, and the evolving digital realm. Each presents a front where the insights we build here will be applied and tested.

Understanding the strategies within the immigration debate is critical, as discussed in Chapter 3, but in our foundational exploration, we acknowledge the need to analyze political rhetoric with a lens capable of cutting through partisan fog and getting to the heart of policy realities.

The trenches of partisanship run deep and the narratives spun within these realms—outlined in Chapter 4—are rich with historical context. However, for the purpose of our introduction, we recognize the importance of overarching operational thought processes that span bipartisan lines, aiming to construct a dialogue rather than deepen divides.

The specter of socialism, outlined in Chapter 5, carries with it a wealth of emotion and history. Before we tackle the myths and realities, we introduce the premise that counters rise from a foundational understanding of the adversary's historical context and current strategies.

Examining the role of faith in American politics, as we do in Chapter 6, requires a grasp on constitutional values and the secular perspectives that often clash with religious rights. Here, we sow the seeds for understanding the dialectic of freedom and faith that underpins this complex debate.

The Second Amendment advocacy, detailed further in Chapter 7, is yet another terrain where understanding multiple perspectives is crucial. At the outset, our goal is to grasp the historical perspectives that inform contemporary challenges without veering into detailed policy discussions.

Amidst the attacks on capitalism, a topic thoroughly explored in Chapter 8, we must first comprehend the adversarial viewpoint as a necessary precursor to defense. The introduction primes us to envision fiscal challenges with an understanding of the subtleties of economic warfare.

The multidimensional landscape of cyber threats demands a sophisticated lens. In Chapter 9, while assessing threats is essential, our immediate task is to understand the adversary's logic, to better fortify our virtual battlements.

Contemplating the global chessboard in Chapter 10 involves discerning the motivations and perspectives of international players. Before we take a deep dive, we anchor ourselves with the realization that understanding these global adversaries aids in projecting American strength effectively.

Medical battlegrounds and the sphere of public health policy, addressed in Chapter 11, require us to dissect the pathogen pathways and political responses from a place of strategic assessment. We prepare ourselves to critique responses while shielding our vantage point from myopic views.

In Chapter 12, we cross swords on educational policy and the preservation of American history and ideals within academia. The dialogue is multifaceted, and our quest begins with setting the stage for an analysis of curricula, controversy, and the art of preserving legacy amidst changing tides.

The chapters ahead will apply this mindset methodically across each arena, providing a comprehensive critique and forward-thinking analysis. Yet, it all starts here, at the genesis of understanding the adversary's mindset. It is from this vantage point that we will embark upon an exploration that stretches across the spectrum of political and strategic thought, rife with fervent discourse and pivotal revelations that could shape the future of our nation.

The goal is not just to layout the battlefield but to grasp the art of intellectual engagement, to stand on the analytical vanguard capable of penetrating partisan barriers and pulling forth the threads of truth and understanding that bind our collective destiny. As we delve into the mind of the adversary, we arm ourselves with the most potent of all tools—knowledge.

Chapter 1:
Decoding the Adversary's Thinking

In our quest to understand the complex tapestry that is our nation's political arena, it's imperative we begin by peeling back the layers of our challenger's logic. Contrary to what you might think, the adversary's mind isn't shrouded in impenetrable mystery, but is often guided by a mosaic of identifiable incentives and historical precedents. By examining the core principles that underpin the opposition's framework, we can start to anticipate their moves, much like a chess player who sees not just the board in front of them but the potential plays and counterplays. It's a dance of intellect and wits, where revealing those predictable patterns becomes our lever to not only comprehend but also to strategically counteract. We stand at the precipice of not just reacting to our adversaries, but outthinking them—moving from a position of defense to one of informed assertiveness that can shape the future discourse of our nation.

Understanding the Opposition's Framework

Is critical for anyone seeking to engage deeply and substantively in the national issues that shape our collective destiny. As we delve into the mindsets that oppose our own, it's imperative to recognize that understanding does not necessarily mean agreement. We can respect the intellectual process that leads to different conclusions, while staunchly defending our positions.

In order to fully comprehend the framework of those with opposing views, one must dissect the core values and beliefs that serve as the foundation for their arguments. Whether it's a different interpretation of economic principles, a unique valuation of social freedoms, or an alternative view on national security, knowing the grounding principles gives insight into the opposition's perspective.

What often goes unrecognized in heated debates is that the opposition's framework is generally built upon its own logical structure. Observing this with an analytical lens allows us to pinpoint where we diverge in our thought processes and ideologies. By understanding these junctions, we can craft more compelling counter-arguments that acknowledge the opposition's stance yet highlight the shortcomings in their position.

Language and narrative play central roles in shaping the framework of any ideology. The words chosen and the stories told are not random; they're calculated to resonate with particular audiences and to paint a vivid picture that aligns with the opposition's views. When we scrutinize the language, we unveil the strategies used to appeal to emotions, fears, and aspirations.

It's also integral to recognize the historical context from which oppositional frameworks arise. The roots of any contemporary belief system can often be traced back to pivotal moments in history. These events have a profound influence on shaping political ideologies and are leveraged by opposition parties to bolster their legitimacy and appeal.

Understanding the methodology behind how these frameworks are disseminated is another key element. Media penetration, educational influences, and grassroots organization are all tools that are utilized to spread and entrench oppositional ideas. By acknowledging these methodologies, one can begin to comprehend how ideas are inculcated within certain sections of society.

When we assess the framework of those who challenge us, we should ask ourselves whether their convictions are based on empirical evidence or if they are bound by the chains of ideological dogmas. This allows us to address the arguments presented with a fact-based counter-narrative, highlighting where emotion has superseded rationality.

Furthermore, the socioeconomic composition of the group which subscribes to the opposition's framework provides us with valuable insights. Groups are not monolithic; they consist of individuals each with their own nuances. Identifying these nuances enables a more personalized approach to discourse, rather than addressing a faceless mass.

A common mistake is to underestimate the opposition, to view their framework through a patronizing lens. However, doing so is at our peril. Many frameworks opposing our own have been honed through challenges, debates, and intellectual rigors. Respect for this process is paramount in truly understanding and effectively challenging these ideas.

Morality and ethics invariably intertwine with political frameworks. The justifications for policy propositions often rest on a moral premise that the opposition holds dear. By dissecting these moral imperatives, we can better comprehend the motives behind policy stances and, when necessary, challenge the ethical consistency of these positions.

It's also essential to grapple with the thought leaders and influencers who mold and shape the opposition's framework. Their writings, speeches, and teachings can provide a window into the ideological heart of the opposition, granting us an opportunity to understand the narrative from its progenitors.

Psychological underpinnings cannot be overlooked. The role of cognitive biases, groupthink, and emotional triggers in shaping political beliefs is substantial. By becoming aware of these elements, we can decipher why certain messages gain traction and others do not — and how to adjust our communication accordingly.

Another aspect to consider is the opposition's vision of the future. What is the endgame for their policies and ideological stances? Envisioning their ideal society allows us to understand the driving forces behind their movements and to highlight potential ramifications that may not have been fully considered.

In essence, to understand the opposition's framework means to engage with it, not as a mere obstacle to be overcome but as a complex set of ideas worthy of examination. This nuanced understanding equips us with the capacity to lead discussions, to influence undecided individuals, and to fortify our own positions with the robustness necessary to withstand rigorous debate.

In closing, our ability to understand the opposition's framework is intrinsically linked to our commitment to the bedrock of democracy: the free exchange of ideas and the respectful contention of beliefs. It is in the crucible of ideological conflict that the strength of our convictions—and our national fabric—is continually forged.

Exploiting the Predictable Patterns

As we continue to scrutinize the adversary's mode of operation, it's crucial to acknowledge the power in identifying and leveraging the patterns they so often rely on. An adversary, whether in the realm of politics, strategy, or broader social engagement, tends to exhibit behavior that, under careful examination, reveals a canvas of repeated strategies and tactical regularities.

In every strategy, from the most benign to the most aggressive, lies a series of actions, decisions, and responses that, due to their nature, become predictable over time. These behaviors follow a sort of script, an algorithmic pathway, honed by years of practice, necessity, or ideology. While these patterns may seem an inevitable trait of any organized group or individual's behavior, they also exist as exploitable vulnerabilities.

Consider a chess player who favors certain opening moves. To the untrained eye, their approach may appear varied and spontaneous. However, to the seasoned opponent, it's a trail of breadcrumbs leading to a trap. This analogy extends to our analysis of political paradigms and actions within our nation's framework. By predicting the opposition's next move, one can effectively counteract or entirely disrupt their agenda.

One of the fundamental ways adversaries betray their predictability is through their language. Political speech, often rife with patterned rhetoric and catchphrases, can clue us into underlying intentions and forewarn us of potential actions. Their language is not merely a tool for communication but a window into their thought processes and future strategies.

Another significant pattern lies in the way adversaries align themselves with certain issues. Observing which topics they lend their voice to, the causes they champion, and those they ignore, speaks volumes to their priorities and subsequent actions. This alignment becomes more evident during moments of national stress or crisis when the stakes are high and true intentions are less cloaked in political correctness.

The predictability of adversaries is also seen in their responses to certain events. Just like muscle memory, they might react impulsively in predictable ways to crises or provocations, adhering to a set of intrinsic guidelines that govern their actions. These responses, if anticipated, can be prepared for and even used to one's advantage when formulating counter-measures.

Furthermore, the tactical patterns of adversaries can often be traced through historical analysis. Studying these archival patterns is not a mere academic exercise; it's akin to unlocking a cipher that allows us to translate their contemporary maneuvers. History doesn't repeat itself, but it often rhymes, as they say, and the echoes can guide us in understanding and predicting current adversary behavior.

On the economic front, adversaries may inadvertently reveal their hand through fiscal policy proposals and spending priorities. Economic initiatives tend to follow a formulaic approach based on underlying philosophies, whether it be austerity, stimulus, or reallocation. By decoding these economic blueprints, one can anticipate the impact of such policies on the larger socio-economic landscape and preemptively formulate counterarguments or policies.

In the sphere of technology and cyber strategies, the patterns become both more sophisticated and more dangerous if left unexploited. Nations and organizations project their strengths and vulnerabilities through their cyber postures, whether they are conscious of it or not. A robust understanding of these digital patterns allows one to shore up defenses and plan offensive measures in the cyber realm that can safeguard or advance national interests.

International relations, too, exhibit characteristic patterns. Geopolitical actions are seldom random; they're more often carefully choreographed steps in a grander dance of power. By perceiving these movements in the international arena as part of a wider pattern, one can position themselves to lead rather than react—setting the stage rather than merely playing a part.

It's important to highlight that while patterns provide insight, it's the discerning application of this knowledge that counts. Identifying a pattern is only the first step. Analysts, strategists, and leaders must carefully weigh when to exploit a predictability and when to stand back, knowing that adversaries can also adapt and evolve, potentially altering their behavior in response to our observations and interventions.

In national politics, legislative and policy-making patterns offer another level of predictability. Examining the trajectories of certain bills, the discourse surrounding them, and their supporters' and detractors' histories can pave the way to understanding regulatory tendencies. This foresight can be instrumental when one is looking to influence policy or prepare for the implications of its enactment.

Moreover, even the patterns of media coverage and information dissemination reveal a trove of exploitable insights. The way news is reported, the stories that gain momentum, and the narratives that get sidelined—all tell a story of prioritization and influence that can be used to predict and shape public perception and discourse.

Lastly, it's crucial to acknowledge the role of human nature in these predictable patterns. The psychological aspects of decision-making, the sway of personal biases, and the impact of collective sentiment often underpin the actions of adversaries. A keen observer can decipher these human elements and anticipate the implications they have for behavior on both individual and group levels.

In conclusion, the potency of predictable patterns cannot be overstated. They stand as a testament to the fact that even within the seemingly chaotic plays of national and international politics, there are discernible rhythms and discernible tactics that, once acknowledged and understood, can be used to steer outcomes. Recognizing these patterns not only serves as a tool for predicting adversary behavior but also empowers proactive stances and robust strategic planning within our nation's ever-evolving narrative.

Chapter 2:
Strategic Foresight: Preparing for the Unseen

Having unpacked the intricate web of an adversary's thought process in the previous chapter, we now pivot to the domain of proactive readiness. In the realm of national issues, the ability to forecast and prepare for potential challenges is more than an art; it's an imperative discipline. Strategic foresight is the chess game played with the pieces of intelligence, long-term planning, and an intuitive grasp of socio-political undercurrents. It's the cultivation of an analytical mindset that doesn't just react to events, but positions itself several moves ahead of them. As we peer through the periscope of proactive governance, we understand that this is not about clairvoyance, but about the meticulous construction of scenarios and responses that align with the currents of change. Within this labyrinth of what-ifs and maybes, the tides turn for those who can anticipate the ripple effects of global actions on the domestic front and preemptively calibrate their strategies to safeguard the nation's interests. Strategic foresight isn't merely a buzzword in a world brimming with unpredictability; it's the navigator's compass ensuring that amidst swelling storms, the ship of state maintains its course toward a horizon of stability and prosperity.

Anticipation Tactics in Modern Politics

The game of politics is no longer a simple contest of ideas; it's a calculated struggle for the hearts, minds, and support of the nation. Winning this battle requires an intricate understanding of your opponent's next move; it demands anticipation tactics that are as dynamic as the ever-changing political landscape. The importance of strategic foresight in politics cannot be overstated, as it allows for the creation of powerful narratives and proactive responses to potential challenges and crises.

Modern politicians and strategists use anticipation tactics to stay ahead of their adversaries. One key approach is through policy forecasting, where teams analyze emerging trends to understand where public policy may need to pivot or hold firm. This skill requires staying attuned to social, economic, and technological developments, and understanding how they might intersect with legislative priorities.

Scenario planning also plays a critical role in anticipation tactics. By envisioning various outcomes based on current events, political players can craft strategies to accommodate different future scenarios. This method demands not only a robust imagination but also a keen analytical ability to assess which imagined scenarios are most probable, and thereby warrant preparedness.

Moreover, message testing is an invaluable tool for gauging public response to policy positions before they are enacted. Using focus groups and opinion polls, political operatives can anticipate backlash or support, allowing for message refinement and the preemptive countering of opposition arguments.

Anticipation tactics are not solely about predicting the future; they're also about creating it. By setting the agenda, politicians can frame the debate on their terms, steering the discourse in a direction that benefits them while catching opponents off guard. Through targeted communication strategies, they can prime the public to receive their policies favorably when they're introduced.

Opponent monitoring is another vital function within anticipation tactics. Teams are assigned to scrutinize public statements, policy proposals, and even internal changes within opposing camps. This intelligence gathering is crucial for anticipating policy shifts and changes in strategic direction by one's political foes.

Similarly, the use of predictive analytics is rising in political campaigns. With access to vast amounts of data, campaigns implement machine learning algorithms to predict voter behavior and respond with appropriate outreach efforts. Through data, predictive trends identify where a campaign should allocate resources for maximum impact.

Coalition forecasting provides further anticipatory insight. By analyzing potential alignments among various interest groups and parties, political strategists can predict and influence how coalitions may form or fracture, thus affecting policy outcomes and election strategies.

Another tactic involves exploiting adversary weaknesses through strategic leaks and information warfare. Politicians and their proxies may leak certain information to test the waters or to discredit opponents, all while officially maintaining plausible deniability.

Roadmapping is also integral to anticipation tactics. Similar to scenario planning, it outlines a path to achieve long-term political goals. Roadmaps must be flexible, allowing for adaptations as circumstances change, yet they are designed with a clear vision that guides immediate actions toward an overarching objective.

Furthermore, the rapid response capability that many modern political organizations have developed is built on anticipatory groundwork. When the unexpected occurs, teams are ready with pre-prepared statements, policy alternatives, or media strategies to control the narrative.

Anticipation also comes into play in legislative battles, where knowing the procedural tactics of opponents can provide a significant advantage. By understanding the rules of the parliamentary game inside and out, politicians can anticipate and block adversary maneuvers, or in some cases, expedite their own agendas.

In the realm of public sentiment, emotional anticipation is crucial. By conducting sentiment analysis, campaigns and officeholders can prepare for shifts in the public mood and adapt their messaging or policy proposals accordingly.

Last but not least, crisis simulations are conducted to prepare for unexpected events such as natural disasters, economic downturns, or political scandals. In these simulations, teams rehearse their responses, refine their communication chains, and ensure that when a real crisis hits, they are not caught unprepared.

From the local council to the corridors of federal power, political battles are fought with a blend of foresight and cunning. Understanding and employing anticipation tactics in modern politics is not just a useful skill; it's an indispensable tool that can mean the difference between being caught off-guard and standing ready to face the future with confidence.

The Role of Intelligence and Counterintelligence

Within the labyrinthine world of strategic foresight, intelligence and counterintelligence emerge as twin pillars that uphold national security. These unseen forces navigate through treacherous terrains, juggling shadowy threats and piercing through deceptive veils to shield the nation's future. Intelligence, in its essential form, serves as the eyes and ears of a state. The intelligence community's intricate work stitches together a tapestry of information—potential threats, adversary capabilities, and strategic vulnerabilities—that policymakers use to craft sound foreign and domestic policy.

Counterintelligence, its necessary counterpart, functions as the shield against espionage, sabotage, and foreign influence. Counterintelligence strategies are meticulously developed to deter, detect, and disrupt the efforts of adversaries attempting to undermine national interests. This work is a perpetual strategic dance; movements must be precise, proactive, and, above all, deeply informed.

In a society that values liberties, the conversation around intelligence operations is often enshrouded with concern over privacy and civil rights. Yet, it is critical to comprehend that intelligence activities are not solely centered on clandestine operations; they also encompass open-source information gathering, which respects legal boundaries while enabling a holistic understanding of global events.

Fostering an analytical perspective, we recognize that intelligence and counterintelligence are not merely about collecting data. They are about discerning patterns, predicting adversary actions, and preemptively nullifying threats. In this complex puzzle, human intelligence (HUMINT), signals intelligence (SIGINT), and cyber intelligence intertwine to form a multilayered defense strategy. It is paramount to adapt and evolve these tactics as adversaries also advance technologically and strategically.

Policymakers rely on intelligence to make informed decisions, often under the immense pressure of impending deadlines and the weight of potential consequences. Intelligence assessments are thus a crucial component in the machinery of decision-making. It helps leaders to navigate the murky waters of international diplomacy, anticipate global crises, and respond appropriately to emerging challenges.

Counterintelligence, while seeming reactive, is intrinsically proactive as well. It is not enough to detect and counteract threats once they have occurred; professionals in this field must penetrate adversarial systems to forecast their intentions and thwart their efforts. It is a high-stakes game of preventing domino effects that could jeopardize national security or, indeed, global stability.

The art of intelligence-gathering and countermeasures is continuously evolving to keep pace with technological advancements. Cyber intelligence, for instance, now plays a pivotal role, as cyber threats have emerged as a significant challenge to national security. In cyberspace, wars are waged invisibly, with hackers and state-sponsored actors attempting to infiltrate critical infrastructure and influence the socio-political landscape.

As nations grow increasingly interconnected, the importance of allies in intelligence work has also escalated. Information sharing among trusted partners enhances collective security and broadens the scope of intelligence, creating an expansive network of shared knowledge poised to neutralize threats before they manifest.

The sterling value of intelligence work, however, also beckons a warning: The very tools and methodologies that fortify a nation against malevolent forces can also be used unethically. The need for oversight is paramount, as the potential for abuse is inherent in any structure wielding such power. Adequate legal and ethical frameworks must be instilled to govern the operations of intelligence communities.

We must also recognize the role of disinformation in counterintelligence. Adversaries often utilize falsified information to deceive, disrupt or destabilize. Counterintelligence efforts, therefore, must include measures to identify and counteract such disinformation, ensuring the public and decision-makers have access to accurate information.

Moreover, the partnership between intelligence agencies and the military is a crucial aspect of national defense. Intelligence serves as the bedrock for military operations, providing situational awareness and tactical advantages. Counterintelligence ensures that these operations are protected from adversarial foreknowledge and interference.

Far from being the sole domain of federal agencies, intelligence and counterintelligence touch upon the everyday lives of citizens. Cybersecurity measures taken by individuals, for instance, contribute to the broader defense against cyber threats. Awareness and educational programs can empower citizens to recognize and report suspicious activities—thus serving as a force multiplier for counterintelligence operations.

Investing in the development and retention of skilled intelligence professionals is non-negotiable. The high-caliber analysis required in both intelligence and counterintelligence roles demands not only acute mental acuity but also emotional intelligence and ethical discernment. Training must, therefore, go beyond technical prowess, encompassing critical thinking, cultural awareness, and ethical decision-making.

In the grand scheme of safeguarding national interests, intelligence and counterintelligence serve as pivotal players in our country's security apparatus. They propagate a state of preparedness, arm policymakers with the requisite knowledge to make prudent decisions, and affirm the nation's commitment to protecting the well-being of its citizens from the unseen dangers that loom on the horizon. In an age where threats are often asymmetric and unconventional, the collective efforts in these domains are indispensable. The foundation laid by their work allows our nation to stand firm against adversaries with both resolve and foresight, safeguarding our values, our security, and our future.

Chapter 3:
Borderline Maneuvers: The Immigration Debate

Navigating through the intricate maze of immigration policy requires more than a cursory understanding of border control; it beckons us to delve into a discussion that's as heated as it is indispensable. The immigration debate is where the rubber of political philosophy meets the hard road of legislative reality. Methods of address must pivot and shift like a skillful diplomat balancing on a wire of national interest and human compassion. Herein, we peel back the layers of political rhetoric that shroud the issue in controversy and examine the tangible impact on neighborhoods, economies, and lives. We dissect how policy and enforcement clash on the ground, shaping an ongoing narrative that influences every facet of American society. This chapter doesn't offer a pedestrian tour of familiar arguments but rather a rigorous test of our collective will to forge a path that honors the diverse tapestry of our nation while maintaining the integrity of our borders.

Analyzing the Political Rhetoric

Dive deep into today's turbulent political climate, and you'll find a kaleidoscope of rhetoric designed to persuade, influence, and sometimes misguide the public. It's essential to dissect this rhetoric to understand the messaging's true impact and intent. In our nation's political discourse, each phrase and word is strategically chosen for maximum effect, but with a keen eye and an analytical mind, one can decode these linguistic maneuvers to reveal the underlying currents of policy and power.

Rhetoric in politics is not a newfound tool but an ancient craft refined over the centuries. It shapes opinions and sways positions on critical issues, from immigration to economic policy. Unraveling the threads of political speech requires a multi-dimensional approach, examining the words themselves, the speakers' history, and the context within which they speak. Political rhetoric often plays on emotions, utilizing pathos to connect with audiences on a personal level.

Encountering political rhetoric first requires an understanding of ethos, the credibility and ethos that a speaker brings to the table. When politicians speak, they don't just present facts or policies; they also weave personal stories and 'evidence' of trustworthiness. This can significantly affect a speech's reception, especially when the public values character as much as, if not more than, the content.

Logos, the logical facet of rhetoric, is often cloaked in statistics, studies, and 'expert' opinions. Politicians deploy these to give weight to their arguments, but this is where critical analysis must rigorously apply. For every figure or fact presented, one must question its origin, methodology, and relevance. Remember, numbers can be potent in making an argument seem irrefutable, but they can also be manipulated or taken out of context.

One of the subtlest tools in political rhetoric is the art of framing. Issues are often presented within a carefully constructed narrative that emphasizes certain aspects while downplaying or ignoring others. The framing of an issue can pre-define the conversation and limit the public's perspective, effectively limiting the scope of debate. Recognizing framing techniques is essential in analyzing political language and its possible manipulations.

Another pivotal element is the use of loaded language - words that carry strong connotations and emotional weight. These powerful words can instantly evoke fear, pride, anger, or any number of emotional responses. Such responses can overshadow rational discussion, making it harder for individuals to make balanced assessments of the issues.

Beyond individual words and phrases, it's crucial to assess the metaphors and analogies politicians use. These comparisons are not chosen at random; they are deliberate devices meant to simplify complex issues and draw parallels to commonly understood concepts. But proceed with caution, for these literary tools can distort as much as they elucidate.

In analyzing the rhetorical landscape, it's also vital to remain aware of omission as a rhetorical strategy. What a politician doesn't say can be just as telling as what they do say. Silence on pressing issues, avoidance of direct questions, or neglecting to address opposing viewpoints can provide insights into underlying agendas and priorities.

The tempo and tone of speech can reveal the emotional temperature of the political moment. Whether it's a calm, collected delivery or a fiery, impassioned plea, the manner in which rhetoric is delivered can affect its reception. Body language, too, is part of this rhetoric, often orchestrated to reinforce verbal messages.

Amid these linguistic strategies, juxtaposition and contrast are frequently employed to create a distinct 'us versus them' narrative. Politicians often frame their positions in direct opposition to an 'other', sometimes turning complex issues into binary choices. This polarizing tactic can solidify support among a base but also contributes to the chasm of division that often characterizes modern politics.

Repetition is another rhetorical staple, used to drill messages into the public's consciousness. Whether it's a campaign slogan or a particular point in a policy argument, repeating specific phrases can engrain them in the collective psyche, sometimes overshadowing their veracity or significance.

Then there's the appeal to tradition or precedent, rhetorically anchoring contemporary issues in historical context to lend them authority. However, this can also blindside individuals to the nuances of today's challenges, as the past is often romanticized or selectively interpreted to bolster current agendas.

Of course, in the digital age, politicians often must tailor their rhetoric for soundbites and social media posts, creating challenges for comprehensive argumentation. The simplification necessary for this environment can be detrimental to nuanced understanding, as complex issues are reduced to hashtags and headlines.

In the same breath, it's essential to recognize the insidious nature of misinformation and "fake news." The rhetorical landscape is not just about what truths are told, but also about the deceptions that are spread. Dissecting fact from fiction becomes an arduous but necessary task for any astute observer of the political scene.

As analysts of political rhetoric, our task is to sift through these complexities with a vigilant, discerning eye. Through critical examination, we can pierce the veil of rhetoric, allowing us to assess the real substance of political positions. It necessitates an unwavering commitment to truth and an understanding that words, while powerful, must be tested against the bedrock of reality.

In conclusion, political rhetoric is a multifaceted instrument wielded with great skill across the spectrum of public dialogue. It is our role to deconstruct these verbal edifices, scrutinizing their foundations and interrogating their forms. By doing so, we ensure that our perspectives remain clear, our discussions rooted in fact, and our convictions born of critical, comprehensive analysis.

Policy and Reality: The Clash on the Ground

Throughout the rigorous debate and the ideological clashes in town halls and on the floors of congress, there lies a palpable disconnect between policy aspirations and the reality on the ground. This chasm is most evident when policies are engineered from high offices yet falter in implementation among the very communities they aim to serve.

The immigration debate, for instance, stands as a stark testament to the divergence between legislative intent and actual impact. While immigration policy is hotly contested in political arenas, the stark realities faced by those on the border - both immigrants and enforcement agencies - speak volumes about the disconnect.

Enforcement officers are often caught in a quagmire of shifting policies that vacillate with the political winds. With every change in administration, the rules of engagement shift, sometimes subtly, sometimes drastically. Thus, the officers on the frontlines must adapt rapidly, yet they also face criticism from all sides for failure to uphold what some deem contradictory mandates.

In communities where immigration policy is felt most acutely, the narrative is far different from the sound bites that echo through congressional halls. Here, locals grapple with the changes in their demographic landscape, the cultural implications, their sense of security, and the economic impact on their daily lives. These constituents bear witness to the fallout of policies that may look good on paper but stumble in practice.

Moreover, small businesses, often touted as the lifeblood of the American economy, have their own tales of hardship when policies on immigration and labor law clash with reality. The challenge of finding skilled labor while navigating a thicket of immigration bureaucracy leaves many business owners caught between a rock and a hard place.

On another front, the warfare waged in the economic realm often sees policies promoting free enterprise and fiscal responsibility yet failing to provide a buffer against the predatory practices of competitors. American businesses face an uphill battle as they strive to compete globally under the heavy hand of regulation that seems to ignore the nuances of international trade warfare.

The Cyber Frontiers, America's new battleground, reveal a similar tale. Policies promising to bolster cyber defenses and protect intellectual property often lag behind the swift and stealthy maneuvers of adversaries. The result is a gaping vulnerability where the reality of cyber-attacks contradicts the assurances of policy.

In the healthcare sector, medical facilities are driven to the brink by policies that do not always translate well in the throes of a crisis. Frontline healthcare professionals deal with the brunt of underfunded programs and sudden policy shifts that often come too late or are ill-fitted for the emergency at hand.

The education system, equally, is no stranger to the discord between policy and practice. Educators navigate constantly evolving standards and curriculum changes that purport to boost academic achievement but may miss the core needs of the student body and the crucial development of critical thinking skills.

The Second Amendment debate also highlights a stark contrast between policy intent and grassroots reality. Law-abiding citizens who view firearm ownership as a foundational right often feel their voices are drowned out by the clamor for regulations that do not necessarily address the complexities of crime or mental health issues tied to gun violence.

Furthermore, global maneuvers that are envisaged in policy circles to project American strength and influence often meet face-to-face with an unpredictable international dynamic. This unpredictability, fueled by cultural misunderstandings and the fog of diplomatic intricacies, can turn well-intended strategies into misadventures.

It's here, on the stark ground of reality, that policy must be tested and adjusted, yet too often the feedback loop is severed by bureaucracy, politics, or ignorance of ground truth. To move forward as a nation, we must forge a closer relationship between those who make the policies and those who live the outcomes.

Indeed, the foundation of American governance was intimacy with reality; the founders constructed a system meant to be agile and responsive to the needs of the governed - a system that today often seems weighed down by its own complexity, jeopardizing that very responsiveness.

As we continue this dialogue, it's critical to remember that while policy may be crafted in the quiet of a legislator's office, its consequences echo loudly in the daily lives of citizens. It is in conscientious reflection, vigorous debate, and a willingness to adapt that the true essence of democracy and responsible governance shines through.

America has always been a nation that not only dreams but achieves. To ensure continued success, the clash between policy and reality should not be viewed as an obstacle, but as an opportunity—a call to engage with the complexities of our time and to refine our ambitions in the unforgiving forge of real-world challenges. It's within this crucible that the promise of America will be realized, or lost, and where we must steadfastly apply our resolve to emerge stronger, more united, and more capable than ever before.

Chapter 4:
In the Trenches of Partisanship

As we turn to Chapter 4, the stark reality of modern American politics reveals itself through the pervasive trenches of partisanship that now define the battlefield. We are witnessing an age where strategic positioning within party lines overshadows the quest for common objectives, often leading to a legislative impasse. This chapter dives deep into the operational tactics that fuel the never-ending game of political chess, dissecting the intense division that has corroded the potential for bipartisanship and mutual progress. Rather than succumbing to the turmoil, this analysis is a call to arms for innovative thought and the reframing of strategies that transcend current practices, urging leaders and citizens alike to muster the foresight and courage to bridge divides. Herein lies the challenge: to understand the intricacies of the opposition's doctrine yet rise above the fray to shape a nation's discourse that is rooted in integrity and fortified by a shared resolve to elevate the common good above the din of partisan warfare.

Operational Thoughts About Bipartisanship

A compelling examination of bipartisanship demands an understanding beyond surface-level calls for unity and cooperation. It's not simply about reaching across the aisle; it's an intricate dance of strategy and philosophy. Bipartisanship conjures up images of legislators working together, setting aside their ideological differences for the common good. While that is the intended portrait, it's imperative to probe deeper and explore what drives our representatives to occasionally blur the partisan lines.

Foremost, we must consider the operational mechanics of bipartisanship. It's a tactical maneuver, often employed to achieve certain legislative goals that would otherwise be unattainable. When a minority seeks to influence the majority's agenda, bipartisanship becomes a pragmatic tool. At other times, majority party members might extend an olive branch to the minority to ensure the passage of legislation, mitigate political risk, or to present a facade of unity on issues deemed important by the public.

The reality is that this political solidarity is not merely about policy but about the power dynamics at play. The value of bipartisanship must be assessed within the context of these power structures. For some, bipartisanship is seen as capitulation, a compromise of core values and principles for the sake of political expediency. For others, it is the linchpin of governance, essential for the passage of any significant legislation in a system as varied and complex as ours.

To navigate these choppy waters, we must discern genuine bipartisanship from its opportunistic counterfeit. True bipartisanship arises from shared interests and common goals; it's a concerted effort that reflects the will and interests of the broader populace. Conversely, the veneer of bipartisanship is often exploited to advance hidden agendas, or to placate dissent within the public sphere, without real collaboration or shared convictions.

In our analysis, we need to dissect key moments in recent history where bipartisanship has either succeeded or failed. What were the conditions that fostered this collaboration? We'll find that crises, whether economic or security-related, often serve as catalysts for bipartisan efforts. It's in these moments of national urgency that party lines may blur, fostering environments where significant compromises become possible – or even necessary.

Furthermore, it's vital to consider the role of leadership in fostering a bipartisan spirit. Political figures who possess the characteristics desirable of statesmen – those who prioritize country over party – can play pivotal roles in rallying support across the aisle. Leadership, in this context, is about vision, integrity, and the ability to articulate a unifying narrative that transcends partisan ideologies.

Yet, we must be cautious not to romanticize bipartisanship. At times, it might be construed as a surrender to mediocrity, where the lowest common denominator dictates policy. This is where the operational thought behind bipartisanship needs to be scrutinized. Does the compromise inherently mean diluting policy to the point of ineffectiveness? Or does it involve sculpting a fine balance that brings forth the best from both ideologies to promote policies that work effectively?

Consider also the cultural implications of bipartisanship. In an age where polarization is often amplified by media echo chambers, instances of bipartisanship can serve as cultural signals, suggesting that collaboration and mutual respect in politics are still possible. Yet, the critical eye must ask if these fleeting moments are sustainable or if they are merely symbolic, transient anomalies in an otherwise fragmented political landscape.

More importantly, successful bipartisanship requires the acknowledgment of shared truths and goals. Without a common factual basis or shared vision for the future, bipartisanship falters before it can even take root. In the current climate of misinformation and divergent realities, finding this common ground is perhaps the most daunting challenge faced by our legislators.

The nexus of bipartisanship revolves around compromise, but not all compromises are created equal. Some serve the greater good, forging resilient policies that stand the test of time, while others are compromises of principle, leading to legislative dead ends or worse—legislation that fails the very people it is supposed to serve.

An operational understanding of bipartisanship thereby requires us to be as circumspect of its failures as we are supportive of its successes. We must acknowledge the difficulty in striking a balance between principled stand and pragmatic governance. Policymakers face an arduous task: how to remain true to their convictions while also working within a pluralistic society that demands cooperation and concessions.

Ultimately, the measure of bipartisanship's value lies in its outcomes. Does the legislation forged in the crucible of bipartisanship stand the test of time? Does it resolve the enduring challenges of our nation? These questions are vital. It's not enough for legislation to pass; it must pass muster with the citizens it impacts, both in the immediacy of the present and in the long annals of the future.

As we venture forward, let's cultivate an analytical perspective on bipartisanship. It's incumbent upon us to peel back the layers, to understand not just the motivations of those who seek bipartisan solutions, but the systemic and cultural underpinnings that either facilitate or hinder such collaborations. In doing so, we gain more than insight into the political process; we gain the foresight to anticipate the ebb and flow of our nation's legislative triumphs and tribulations.

Restrained by realism yet inspired by the potential of unity, our journey through the operational thoughts about bipartisanship is one of cautious optimism. It is a nuanced stance that recognizes the complexity of governing a diverse nation, advocating neither for blind compromise nor unyielding partisanship, but the judicious application of both, in service of the Republic.

The Republican Critique of Democratic Strategies

Delves into an analytical exploration of the strategies employed by the Democratic Party from the perspective of their opposition. The Republican viewpoint characterizes these strategies as flawed in their conception and delivery, arguing that they often stem from an ideological framework that prioritizes progressive agendas over pragmatic governance.

In dissecting the Democratic strategies, Republicans frequently point out what they perceive as a disconnect between campaign promises and policy efficacy. The GOP contends that Democrats prioritize short-term political gains through populist rhetoric, which they argue overlooks the need for sustainable, long-term solutions to complex issues. The focus on charismatic leadership and emotional appeal, from a conservative standpoint, can obscure insufficient policy depth and execution.

Critics within the Republican Party often argue that Democratic fiscal policies reflect a lack of economic restraint. They claim that the liberal approach to budgeting and government spending leads to excessive national debt and burdens future generations with financial liabilities. The Republican establishment advocates for fiscal conservatism, emphasizing the importance of reducing government intervention in the economy as a vital component of national prosperity.

On the topic of national security, Republican critiques highlight what they see as a tendency for Democrats to underappreciate the importance of a robust military presence and a firm approach to international affairs. From a conservative vantage point, Democratic strategies sometimes signal weakness to adversaries by prioritizing diplomatic engagement over deterrent strength.

Republicans also take issue with the Democratic Party's stance on immigration, castigating it as overly permissive and harmful to the country's social and economic fabric. The GOP underscores the need for stronger border control and immigration policies that prioritize merit, legality, and assimilation into American cultural norms.

Healthcare remains another contentious front, where Republicans allege that Democratic approaches — such as the push for a single-payer system — compromise the quality of care, stifle competition, and strip citizens of choice. Echoing the virtues of free-market solutions, the GOP asserts that competition leads to innovation and improved access to healthcare services.

Scrutinizing social policies, conservative critics argue that Democratic strategies often promote a culture of dependency rather than self-reliance. Republican commentators suggest that social welfare programs should be structured with the aim of temporary assistance and incentivization of workforce participation to promote individual prosperity and reduce the reliance on government sustenance.

When discussing the realm of education, Republicans argue that Democratic strategies frequently encroach on educational freedom and parental rights. They claim that the call for universal pre-K and community college, while well-intentioned, falls short of addressing core issues like education quality and the preservation of choice in schooling. They espouse a vision where voucher programs and charter schools are given prominence as paths to educational innovation and diversity.

Republican critiques extend into environmental policy, where they accuse the Democratic Party of embracing extreme measures that threaten economic stability, like the Green New Deal. Instead, Republicans tend to favor an approach that balances environmental stewardship with economic development, advocating for energy independence and the responsible use of natural resources.

Labor and employment strategies have also been a point of contention, with Republicans criticizing Democratic support for increased unionization and what they see as excessive regulation of the labor market. GOP analysts argue that such strategies can hinder economic growth and job creation, advocating instead for pro-business policies they believe stimulate the economy.

Within the field of civil liberties, Republicans cast a wary eye on what they perceive as Democratic policies that stretch the bounds of government power, particularly in relation to gun rights, freedom of speech, and religious liberties. Republicans stake a firm claim in protecting constitutional rights and often see Democratic strategies as infringing upon these core American freedoms.

On foreign policy, Republican observers counter Democratic strategies with skepticism toward international agreements and organizations that, in their view, might compromise American sovereignty. They advocate for a stronger assertion of American interests and a more guarded approach to international commitments.

Republican criticism doesn't stop at domestic and foreign policies; it extends into perceptions of governance style. The GOP paints a picture of Democratic leadership as tending toward overcentralization of power, bureaucratic expansion, and regulatory overreach, which they believe constricts individual liberty and stifles entrepreneurial initiative.

Crucially, Republicans argue that Democratic strategies often exhibit an urban-centric bias and an insufficiency in addressing rural concerns, which leads to a disconnection with a significant segment of the American populace. The criticism extends to what is seen as an elitist attitude toward Middle America and traditional values, allegedly eschewed by coastal and urban Democratic strongholds.

Finally, Republican critics of Democratic strategies emphasize the importance of analyzing policies through a lens of national unity and cohesion. They argue that a nation's strength lies in its shared values and ideals, suggesting that bipartisan efforts should prevail over partisan maneuvering. From their perspective, Democratic strategies can sometimes polarize and divide rather than unify, underscoring the need for an approach that aligns with America's foundational principles of liberty, equality, and justice for all.

Chapter 5:
The Socialist Threat: Myths and Realities

Continuing from the sharp critique of partisanship, we venture into perhaps one of the most provocative arenas of political discourse: the purported 'socialist threat'. Grappling with a topic that's fired up countless debates, it's crucial to peel away layers of hyperbole to isolate fact from fiction. What's often branded as socialist incursion in America garners attention and stirs a sense of urgency, but is there substance behind the spectacle? This chapter dares to dissect the Marxist misconceptions and, equipped with a fine-tuned lens, examines the underpinning realities of these assertions. By delving into the ideological mechanics, we stitch together a narrative that appraises socialist ideology against our nation's staunch conservative principles and retraces the footprints of socialism throughout our history. It's a pursuit to break down the barriers of misapprehension and to realign the conversation with the bedrock of truth—reminding us that in the grand tapestry of ideological battlefields, knowledge and nuance stand as our most formidable weapons.

The Marxist Agenda in America Today

Iis a topic of intense debate and scrutiny. In the current American political landscape, claims of Marxism often surface in heated dialogues, with voices on one side positing that Marxist ideology is stealthily infiltrating various spheres of the United States, particularly in the realms of education, culture, and economics. To unpack this conversation, it is essential to scrutinize the origins of Marxist thought and pinpoint where these ideas manifest in contemporary society.

Marxism, at its core, is a socio-economic ideology that critiques capitalism and proposes a classless society, where resources and means of production are commonly owned. The allure of such an ideology has long been debated in American history, with periods of heightened interest especially noted during times of socio-economic strife. Today, the echoes of this theoretical framework reverberate through discussions on wealth distribution, healthcare, and labor rights.

One of the primary arenas where Marxist ideology is accused of taking hold is in the American educational system. Critics assert that curriculums and academic discourse are increasingly being shaped by principles that align with Marxist philosophy. They argue this is particularly evident in the areas of social justice, critical theory, and historical analysis, where traditional American values are sometimes challenged in favor of exploring historical materialism and class struggle.

Further, the realm of cultural production is said to be saturated with Marxist concepts. This is seen in the push for deconstructing traditional narratives and promoting media that centers on class conflict, anti-capitalist sentiment, and revolutionary ideals. Advocates for this perspective assert that the entertainment industry and the overarching culture industry are potent vehicles for disseminating these concepts to the broader population.

In economics, the call for increased government intervention and regulation, universal healthcare, and welfare programs is often labeled as Socialist or Marxist. Proponents of conservative economic principles argue that such measures epitomize the gradual erosion of the free market and individual entrepreneurship that are foundational to America's economic success.

It is essential to differentiate between social democracy, a system that seeks to democratize the economy while still retaining a capitalist framework, and Marxism, which ultimately aims for a revolution that eradicates capitalism entirely. Critics often conflate progressive policies with Marxist intentions, creating a misrepresentation that fuels division and misunderstanding.

The debate intensifies when discussing labor unions and worker rights; areas where Marxism places intrinsic value. The recent resurgence of unionization efforts in corporate entities across America is a reflection of a renewed focus on worker's rights. This movement espouses some Marxist sentiments about the power dynamics between employers and employees and the right to collective bargaining.

The perception of Marxism in America is further complicated by geopolitical events. Relations with countries that openly embrace or are perceived to support Marxist ideologies impact domestic politics and fuel suspicions about internal subversion or ideological infiltration.

Despite these concerns, it is critical to evaluate the actual prevalence of Marxism in American policies and social changes. The dominant economic system in the U.S. remains staunchly capitalist, with private ownership and market competition continuing to thrive. The specter of Marxism, for many, serves more as a rhetorical device to express fear over certain social reforms rather than a measurable shift in the country's foundational economic structure.

A nuanced discussion about the influence of Marxist thought in America cannot ignore the existing disparities and discontent that might draw individuals towards more radical ideologies. Disparities in wealth and opportunity, perceived injustice, and lack of social mobility provide fertile ground for alternative ideologies to take root in the collective consciousness of society.

Challenging the American Marxist narrative requires a robust reaffirmation of the principles that undergird the nation's constitution and history. Advocates of this approach admonish the necessity of upholding the values of individual liberty, private property, and the pursuit of happiness – foundational elements which they assert are antithetical to Marxist doctrine.

This sub-section aims not to sow divides but to encourage critical examination of the claims surrounding the Marxist agenda in America. By systematically disentangling fact from hyperbole, individuals develop a more profound comprehension of the genuine threats, if any, that exist. This comprehension allows for more cogent argumentation and policy development that upholds America's ideals.

Ultimately, the discussion of Marxist influence in America is not only about policies and economics but also about the underlying philosophical beliefs regarding human nature, governance, and societal organization. The crucial question is whether these beliefs will harmonize with America's long-standing traditions or set the stage for a radical transformation of the nation's identity.

In the end, the discourse on Marxism in America reflects a broader conversation about the future direction of the nation. It's a dialogue that juxtaposes continuity against change, freedom against equality, and tradition against reform. The course of America's journey is a testament to its resilience and capacity for evolution, always striving to forge a society that upholds the ideals of its founding while navigating the currents of contemporary ideological shifts.

As America strides into the future, the narrative around Marxism will continue to evolve. It's a complex mosaic that intertwines political, economic, and cultural threads. Vigilance and perspicacity are required from every social actor to ensure that the values which have propelled the nation to prosperity continue to be honored and advanced.

Countering Socialist Narratives with Conservative Principles

In the ongoing ideological battle that shapes the American political landscape, there is a profound necessity to address and counter socialist narratives. Yet, to engage in this sophisticated discourse, it's imperative that one possesses a firm grasp of conservative principles, which offer practical and visionary alternatives. Constructing an effective counterargument means dissecting socialist arguments, revealing their flaws, and presenting conservative ideals that not only solve problems but also promote personal liberty and economic freedom.

At the forefront of the socialist narrative is the call for economic equality, often expressed as a quest to eliminate the disparities between the haves and have-nots. Socialists frame this quest in moral terms, presenting it as a fight for justice. However, conservatives counter by emphasizing that equality of opportunity, not outcome, is the key to a fair society. Conservatives argue for a system that provides everyone with the chance to succeed based on merit, hard work, and innovation, which in turn fosters a more dynamic and prosperous society.

Another cornerstone of socialist rhetoric is the demand for expanded government control and oversight in virtually every sector of society. Conservatives challenge this perspective with the principle of limited government, proposing that the most effective government is one that empowers individuals and communities to make decisions for themselves. They assert that bureaucracy hampers innovation and efficiency, and that a bloated government leads to overreach and encroachment on individual freedoms.

Socialists often advocate for universal healthcare, claiming it as a fundamental right for all. Conservatives, while acknowledging the need for a robust and accessible healthcare system, advocate for market-based solutions. They believe competition drives quality up and costs down and that government-run systems suffer from inefficiency and degraded service. They push for reforms that enhance choice and control for patients and doctors alike.

The protection of labor interests is another theme woven into socialist narratives. While conservatives agree on the dignity of work, they support the free-market economy's ability to fairly negotiate wages and employment terms without excessive government intervention. They see union overreach and stringent labor laws as stifling to both economic freedom and growth, advocating instead for policies that encourage entrepreneurship and job creation.

Socialist narratives often portray capitalism as inherently exploitive, and call for redistributive economic policies to combat corporate greed. In contrast, conservatives uplift the free market as the greatest engine of prosperity the world has ever known. They argue that capitalism rewards innovation and efficiency and that wealth redistribution undermines the incentive for wealth creation that benefits society at large.

On the environmental front, socialist agendas typically support rigid regulations and government-led initiatives to combat climate change. Conservatives, while recognizing the importance of stewardship over the environment, promote balanced approaches that do not cripple economic growth. They advocate for market-driven environmentalism, where innovation and private-sector solutions lead to sustainable practices and technological advancements.

Educationally, socialism often encourages a state-centric model, where government directs learning standards and outcomes. Conservatives argue for parental choice and local control, believing that competition among educational institutions yields higher quality and empowers parents to select the best learning environment for their children. They also emphasize the importance of maintaining historical and civic education to foster informed and responsible citizens.

Concerning welfare, socialists propose extensive social safety nets and governmental assistance programs. Conservatives do not reject the need for a safety net but argue for programs that incentivize work and self-sufficiency, fearing that long-term dependency on the state is detrimental to the individual's potential and dignity. They advocate for reforms that help individuals transition from welfare to work, emphasizing personal responsibility and community support.

The topic of national defense also showcases sharp contrasts between socialist and conservative ideologies. Socialists may criticize military spending and advocate for reallocating funds toward social programs, while conservatives emphasize the importance of a strong national defense to ensure peace and stability. They advocate for a well-resourced military that can protect national interests and maintain global security.

Lastly, the debate over individual rights and freedoms is central to the confrontation between socialist narratives and conservative principles. Socialists often frame government intervention as necessary for protecting the public good, which can lead to infringement of personal liberties. Conservatives staunchly defend constitutional rights and freedoms, such as free speech, the right to bear arms, and religious liberty, advocating for a society where the government protects these rights instead of diminishing them.

These contrasting views establish a framework for debate and discussion that is crucial for the health of American democracy. Conservative principles offer avenues to counter socialist narratives by promoting a society characterized by freedom, responsibility, and enterprise. By outlining, understanding, and articulating these principles clearly, conservatives can present a compelling vision that resonates with the American values of liberty and individualism.

In grappling with these complex issues, it's essential that the discourse remains respectful and evidence-based. Policy should not be shaped by emotion or ideological purity but rather by what works in practice to uplift the most people while preserving the principles upon which the nation was founded. By engaging in thoughtful and informed debate, conservatives can demonstrate that their principles not only provide effective counterpoints to socialist narratives but also lay the groundwork for a flourishing and prosperous society.

In the end, the strength of conservative principles lies not merely in their opposition to socialist ideas but in their positive vision for society. They seek to empower the individual, unleash human potential, and nurture a culture of achievement and innovation. As we move forward, it is these principles that will guide us toward a future marked by freedom, prosperity, and the relentless pursuit of happiness that defines the American spirit.

Chapter 6:
Faith and Freedom: God in American Politics

As we segue from examining socialist influences to dissecting the spiritual landscape, Chapter 6 unravels the profound intertwining of faith with the fabric of American governance. In the United States, where the quest for liberty is often seen through a spiritual lens, the discourse on divine providence isn't just sugar-coated idealism—it's a potent historical force. Religion courses through the nation's veins, from the inscriptions on our currency to the oaths that bind our officials. This analysis isn't about proselytization or presenting a homily; it's an imperative look at how faith and freedom play a consequential role in the righteous arena of American politics. Can we fully comprehend the path of a nation without considering the faith of its people? This chapter doesn't just nod at the past; it delves into how current policy and civic interaction are in a constant dance with religious underpinnings. It's a dance that impacts everything from legislative priorities to grassroots activism—a testament to the enduring legacy of faith-based values in the quest for freedom and justice within the star-spangled tapestry we strive to comprehend.

The Constitutional Cornerstone: Faith-Based Values

As we pivot from the exploration of socialism's encroachment to a broader understanding of America's political scene, we must delve into a foundational element of the nation's fabric: faith-based values. At the heart of the American Constitution lies an implicit acknowledgment of religious influence. These values are, without doubt, the bedrock upon which many of our laws and societal norms rest. Now, let's explore how these faith-based principles have shaped our country and continue to act as a compass in an ever-evolving political landscape.

The Framers of the Constitution, diversely influenced by their individual beliefs and the philosophical undertones of the Enlightenment, recognized the importance of freedom in religious practice. Their fresh memories of a Europe plagued with religious persecution birthed the First Amendment. This pivotal aspect of the Bill of Rights guarantees each individual the liberty to worship as they choose or to not worship at all—showcasing the Framers' intention for religious plurality and tolerance.

However, while ensuring the separation of church and state, it is pivotal to acknowledge that religious principles did provide moral guidance. Our legal systems and institutions are indelibly informed by a Judeo-Christian ethic that values life, liberty, and the pursuit of happiness—principles that resonate deeply within the majority of all major world religions.

Moreover, faith-based communities have historically rallied for social changes that echo the moral teachings of their sacred texts. Think of the abolitionist movement, women's suffrage, and the civil rights era—all interwoven with deeply spiritual undertones and figures who used the language of faith to fight for justice. One cannot examine these pivotal moments in American history without recognizing the role faith played in shaping these national transformations.

In contemporary politics, faith voices continue to be powerful, sometimes polarizing, forces in public discourse. They advocate for policies ranging from pro-life legislation to immigration reform, grounded in compassion and human dignity. The salience of such issues speaks volumes—it shows that faith-based values, while sometimes controversial, animate passionate social and political engagement.

It is essential to realize that America's legal and value system advocates not for one faith tradition but instead for each individual's, or community's, right to hold faith. This is where the interplay of personal conviction and public policy becomes complex and, at times, contentious. Those at the helm of political thought and action must navigate this labyrinth with care and respect for the multifaceted tapestry of belief that composes the United States.

Faith-based values also play an instrumental role in volunteerism and charity work. Many faith organizations provide essential social services and humanitarian relief—areas where sometimes government alone cannot reach or refuses to tread. The altruistic endeavors of faith communities substantially contribute to societal welfare and manifest the compassion at the heart of many religions.

Yet, critics argue that the incorporation of faith into politics invariably leads to division. Some fear that fostering a religiously infused political atmosphere can inadvertently marginalize those who do not share the majority's beliefs, or worse, engender legislation that infringes upon personal freedoms. Indeed, maintaining a delicate balance where faith informs but does not dominate political decision-making is no trivial task.

The present dialogue on faith and politics also witnesses arguments that secularism is sometimes intolerantly enforced, underestimating the positive role faith can have in public life. Thus, there exists a challenging dichotomy that requires discerning judgment and prudence. The beauty and the struggle of American democracy is in managing these tensions—where space is given for both faith expression and secular governance.

This balance is not static but dynamic, requiring continuous dialogue and reassessment as our nation grows in diversity and complexity. Policies and laws must adapt to reflect this living reality, honoring the past's wisdom while boldly addressing today's unique challenges. In this endeavor, faith-based values can provide a guiding light without becoming an overpowering force that dims the glow of others.

Digging deeper, it becomes apparent that the core American values—such as integrity, hard work, and community service—are intrinsically linked to the religious tenets professed by many of its citizens. These values, when harnessed positively, can lead to robust national character and governance that acknowledges a higher accountability—a sentiment that resonates with both religious and secular individuals alike.

With the objective of maintaining and nurturing a richly diverse, inclusive democratic society, it is imperative for leaders to understand the impact of faith-based values on American life. It is not a matter of prioritizing one belief system over another but rather embracing the mosaic of our national ethos in which these values occupy a significant place.

As the nation continues to grapple with pressing issues, our collective understanding must expand beyond the divisive rhetoric to appreciate the unifying potential of faith-based values. In times of division, returning to foundational values offers a firm ground for re-engagement and common purpose. It is in these values that Americans can find commonality and the resolve to forge a more perfect union.

In conclusion, faith-based values are not just the threads in America's historic tapestry; they are active and vibrant strands in the fabric of today's society. Their colors, textures, and patterns add depth and richness to the national narrative. As we venture further into the twenty-first century, these principles continue to shape dialogues, inspire movements, and remind us of the spirit that birthed a nation committed to freedom, justice, and the inherent dignity of all people.

Religious Rights and the Secular Response –

The landscape of American politics is a terrain marked by the interplay of diverse beliefs and secular ideologies. As we navigate the terrain laid out in the previous chapters, we hone in on the delicate balance between faith and freedom in the fabric of the nation. At the core of the First Amendment lies the essence of religious liberty, an element so fundamental that it shapes the heartbeat of America. Yet, in an era where secularism is gaining ground, we witness a peculiar tension playing out on this stage of liberties and rights.

The foundation of religious liberty encompasses the right to practice one's faith without fear of persecution or undue interference. This principle seems straightforward, but it is routinely contested by secular forces that argue for a stricter delineation between church and state. They view religious expressions, especially when intertwined with the public domain, as incursions into a zone that ought to remain neutral – which means free from religious influences.

The secular response to the upward trend of religious advocacy has been multifacetal. One aspect is the push for laws and policies that ensure governmental neutrality and the prevention of what is perceived as state endorsement of religion. This calls for a constant scrutiny of legislations, judicial rulings, and executive pronouncements, measuring them against the yardstick of the Establishment Clause.

Amidst these legal skirmishes, educational settings have become a battleground. The debate on whether religious instruction, symbols, or observances should be allowed in public schools exposes the fault lines between what is considered an individual's right to freedom of religion and the establishment of a secular educational norm.

In the healthcare sector, the clash surfaces in terms of conscience rights versus patient access to services like contraception and abortion, with fervent arguments championed on both sides. While one camp vociferously protects the sanctity of life as they see it, the secular perspective pits individual choice and the provision of comprehensive healthcare above religious constraints.

At the heart of this discourse, there's a burgeoning narrative that paints religious rights as a counterforce to progressive values. The claim is that under the guise of religious freedom, there are attempts to undermine rights relating to gender, sexuality, and equality. The secular argument unfolds, contending that religious freedom should not be a license to discriminate.

Controversies surrounding public expressions of faith, such as prayer in government meetings or religious monuments on public land, reflect a broader unease. These instances often become litmus tests for how society balances heritage and inclusivity, the past and the evolving present. And while some view these as harmless manifestations of a majority faith, others see them as exclusionary symbols that divide rather than unite.

Amid this contentious dialogue, a discerning examination of historical precedents can ground the conversation. The Founding Fathers grappled with these very issues, framing a constitution that both protected religious expression and prevented the establishment of a national creed. Their vision of religious freedom was not only intended for the protection of the dominant faith but as a safe harbor for all faiths and beliefs.

The percolation of faith into the political realm is an evident reality. Politicians often invoke divine favor, make policy decisions with religious undertones, and even integrate faith into their electoral strategy. The secular viewpoint fiercely refutes the idea of faith influencing policy, advocating for policies based on reason, empirical evidence, and universality over religious doctrine.

Navigating these stormy waters requires a negotiation of values, an understanding that secularism and religious liberties need not be antagonists but can coexist within a framework of mutual respect and understanding. The goal shouldn't be one overshadowing the other but rather, a synergy that respects the diversity of beliefs and the neutrality of the state.

Legal challenges, from cake-baking disputes to employment decisions based on faith, serve as microcosms of the broader issue. Each case, with its unique narrative, becomes a thread in the tapestry of this ongoing national discourse, a tapestry that's being scrutinized more closely than ever by the courts, the legislature, and the public.

As secular advocacy groups mobilize for greater separation of church and state, religious organizations also fortify their defenses. They contend that the free exercise of religion extends into public life and that a secular society need not stifle the visibility of faith. This tug-of-war is reflective of not just legal interpretations, but deeply entrenched worldviews.

The secular pushback against religious rights does not come without its own paradigm of tolerance and understanding. Here lies the paradox: the defense of secularism is often mounted with as much fervor as the zeal of the religiously devout. It is a quest to redefine boundaries in an ever-shifting landscape of cultural norms and values.

In the grand scheme of things, it's essential to acknowledge that both religious rights and secular responses are born out of a shared commitment to individual liberty. They each stem from a desire to uphold a vision of America that reflects their ideals. But the ultimate test will be whether these disparate convictions can anchor themselves in a conversation that promotes conciliation rather than polarization— an America where everyone can peacefully coexist despite profound disagreements.

Thus, in the theater of America's future, the contestation between religious rights and secularism will surely continue to be a cornerstone of societal evolution. The balancing act will persist, the debates will undoubtedly wax and wane, but in the end, what must prevail is a resolve to respect diversity, protect individual liberties, and embrace the breadth of human conscience and reason within the democratic framework that has been handed down to us.

Chapter 7:
The Right to Bear Arms:
Understanding 2A Advocacy

Inherently woven into the fabric of American principles, the right to bear arms stands as a testament to the enduring belief in individual sovereignty and the deterrence of tyranny. Our exploration into 2A advocacy unveils not just a constitutional right, but a cultural emblem that galvanizes citizens towards vigilance and liberty. Synthesizing historical context with contemporary fervor, this chapter delves into the origins of the Second Amendment and its pivotal role in shaping American identity. We dissect the keen strategies utilized by advocates to fortify this cornerstone, steadily confronting modern challenges while navigating the turbulent terrain of legislative adversarial tactics. The heartfelt stories of commitment from the broader community underscore a profound relationship between a nation and its arms—a symbol of a free people's resolve to protect their way of life, their families, and their future against any encroachments upon their freedoms.

Historical Perspectives on the Second Amendment

Turning our attention to a cornerstone of American constitutional dialogue, understanding the origin and evolution of the Second Amendment is essential. This amendment, part of the Bill of Rights, has been a subject of intense scrutiny, debate, and veneration since its inception. Born out of a historical context steeped in the quest for liberty and self-governance, the Second Amendment was ratified in 1791, guaranteeing the right of the people to keep and bear arms.

At the crux of this right lay the experiences of the Founding Fathers who had lived through the tyranny of a distant crown. Their experiences with British rule left them with a strong belief in the need for a militia to safeguard the state's freedom and for individuals to protect themselves and their families. It's imperative to acknowledge the volatile world of colonial America where self-defense was not merely conceptual but often a stark reality. Without the individual's right to bear arms, reliance on the government for personal safety was tantamount to the dependence they had fought so rigorously to escape.

In the vein of protecting liberty, the Second Amendment also reflected a mistrust of permanent, standing armies, which could be tools of oppression. The well-regulated militia referenced in the text was thought to counteract this potential threat. Historically, militias comprised everyday citizens ready to defend their communities against both domestic and foreign adversaries.

Much of the early debate around the Second Amendment rested on the balance between state and federal power. The proponents of a strong centralized government (Federalists) clashed with those who advocated for states' rights (Anti-Federalists), with the latter fearing that federal overreach could lead to the very tyranny they had fought against.

In the 19th century, the interpretation of the Second Amendment continued to evolve. With the expansion of the frontier and the lawlessness that often dominated those territories, the individual's right to bear arms became synonymous with the pioneering spirit, seen not as merely a right but a necessity.

As the nation moved into the 20th century, technological advances introduced new types of firearms, and the country faced novel challenges. Organized crime during Prohibition, for example, stirred a debate that led to the National Firearms Act of 1934, regulating certain types of weapons.

The next pivotal moment in the history of the Second Amendment was the landmark case District of Columbia v. Heller in 2008. The United States Supreme Court held that the amendment protects an individual's right to possess a firearm for lawful purposes, such as self-defense within the home. This ruling marked a significant shift in the legal understanding of the Second Amendment, asserting that the right was not solely tied to militia service.

Following this precedent, the legal landscape continued to be shaped by further interpretations and rulings. However, not only judicial perspectives but also cultural narratives played a key role in framing the dialogue around the Second Amendment. The rise of the civil rights movement, for instance, emphasized self-defense as not only a constitutional right but also a human right, especially during times when the government failed to protect certain communities.

The amendment's wording, with its mention of militias and the right to keep and bear arms, remains a focal point in this debate. Critics often point out the need for regulation and concerns about public safety, while advocates emphasize the historical context that underscores a fundamental liberty.

Understanding the Second Amendment requires a balanced comprehension of history, law, and societal change. It's a testament to the living nature of the U.S. Constitution—a document designed to be both immutable in principle and adaptable in practice. Yet, questions persist about where the line between individual rights and collective security should be drawn.

In conclusion, the longevity and dynamism of the Second Amendment discussions reflect continuously evolving American values. Historical perspectives on this amendment uncover a tapestry of intentions, interpretations, and implications that echo through legal, social, and political realms. As the nation forges ahead, the debates surrounding the Second Amendment will inevitably continue, shaped by the ever-changing landscape of American society, yet invariably rooted in the historical groundwork laid by the nation's founders.

With this foundation of historical perspective, it's essential to embark on a deeper analysis of the modern challenges and adversarial tactics that now face the Second Amendment and its advocacy in contemporary America, ever-relevant in our pursuit of understanding the nation's ongoing constitutional conversation.

Modern Challenges and Adversarial Tactics

In the arena of Second Amendment rights, the landscape is fraught with modern challenges that trigger adversarial tactics with unyielding fervor. The right to bear arms stands as a testament to the nation's constitutional bedrock, yet its place in contemporary society is hotly contested, demanding a vigilant and strategic response from advocates.

One of the spearheads of the modern challenge is the evolution of firearms themselves. As technology advances, so too does the complexity of weapons. This has resulted in an arms race, not between nations, but within the very fabric of the community. Advocates face the daunting task of separating the wheat from the chaff — promoting responsible ownership while staunchly opposing the misuse of advanced weaponry.

Moreover, adversarial tactics have evolved, employing social media and the internet as platforms for propaganda and misinformation. It's a war of bytes and beliefs where advocates must counter with facts and well-reasoned arguments that acknowledge the legitimacy of concerns while standing firm on constitutional rights.

Legislation remains a battlefield, with lobbying efforts intensifying from both sides of the debate. Privacy concerns over background checks and registration databases culminate in a standoff concerning individual liberties, surveillance, and the common good. Advocates of 2A rights must navigate this complex web of privacy rights, grafting the preservation of liberty onto the steadfast branch of national security.

Adversaries also deploy emotional narratives centered on tragedy and loss to sway public opinion — methodical strategies designed to tug at heartstrings and circumvent rational argumentation. In this passionate outpouring, 2A proponents must balance compassion with clarity, articulating the undiluted value of self-defense and deterrence within the rule of law.

A unique modern challenge is the shifting cultural perception of gun ownership. As urbanization and technological progress march on, a gap widens, distancing citizens from the traditions and practicalities that once made firearm proficiency commonplace. Advocates now educate and remind society of the historical and current relevance of the constitutionally enshrined right to bear arms, instilling a culture of respect and responsibility.

Seen from the judiciary perspective, the debate takes on a more complex dimension. Landmark court cases ascend to the upper echelons of judicial scrutiny, yet the interpretation hinges upon a spectrum of philosophies — from originalism to a living constitution approach. Defenders of the Second Amendment thus engage in intellectual combat, interpreting Founder's intentions while grounding arguments in contemporary application.

International influences further muddy the waters as global perceptions and policies regarding gun control seep into the American psyche. Advocates must therefore assert national sovereignty, upholding the uniqueness of the American experiment amidst an array of foreign regulatory frameworks.

Enforcement and compliance introduce another arena where opponents scrutinize every misstep. Second Amendment protectionists must advocate for fair and consistent enforcement practices that don't disproportionately impact or alienate specific communities, synthesizing a balanced approach between safety and the exercise of rights.

Mental health emerges as a joint concern, bridging the divide with a shared desire to prevent those deemed a danger to themselves or others from possessing firearms. This common ground, however, is fraught with disagreement over criteria and processes, prompting 2A advocates to engage thoughtfully in the discourse of health and rights intertwined.

In the halls of academia and media, the narrative often paints a somber picture of gun ownership, introducing biases that demonize firearms and their advocates. In response, pro-2A factions strive to empower through education, debunking myths and presenting a balanced narrative that honors both the individual and collective components of the Second Amendment.

Reinvigorating the grassroots, 2A supporters inject vigor into the public square, mobilizing citizens who believe in the right of self-preservation. They navigate the fine line of fostering community sentiment without bowing to the pitfalls of extremism or alienation that adversaries often anticipate and exploit.

Emerging technologies such as 3D-printed firearms and "ghost guns" without serial numbers present unforeseen legal and ethical dilemmas, providing adversaries with ammunition to advocate for restrictive policies, while proponents are compelled to tackle the implications of innovation that circumvent traditional control systems.

Within the financial sector, adversaries have begun to exert pressure, as corporations and financial institutions adopt policies that scrutinize firearm-related transactions. This economic encroachment into the realm of rights instigates a dialogue on corporate influence and the profound need to protect legal commerce from ideological constriction.

As America progresses into an era of unprecedented challenges, those who stand guardians to the Second Amendment confront adversarial strategies with determination. It's a dynamic theater where tactics are as diverse as the populace itself, requiring agility, insight, and unshakable commitment. Amid such strife, the sanctity of foundational principles must be upheld, taught, and passed on, for these rights define the essence of liberty and empower citizens to stand as their own defenders — today, tomorrow, and for generations yet to come.

Chapter 8:
Economic Warfare: Capitalism Under Siege

The very essence of the American Dream, powered by the grinding gears of capitalism, finds itself encircled by strategic forces aiming to dismantle its core. As we draw the battle lines of economic warfare, it's crucial to scrutinize every maneuver that threatens the sanctum of free enterprise. American capitalism, a beacon of innovation and prosperity, is not merely in a contest over market shares but in a fierce struggle for its foundational principles. Challenges arising from global competitors, wielding state-run economics as a weapon, force us to re-evaluate our strategies to safeguard our economic interests. The encroachment of socialist ideologies into the fabric of our financial systems reveals a stark contrast to the pillars of individual liberty and private ownership. In this chapter, we dissect the assaults on capitalistic frameworks and fortify our understanding of defending a system that has lifted countless individuals from the clutches of poverty to the pinnacle of progress. While we stand vigilant against external economic aggressors, we must also purge the internal decay of complacency and ignite the unyielding spirit of entrepreneurial courage to ensure the vitality of capitalism remains unassailable in the face of modern-day economic combat.

Envisioning the Fiscal Challenges from an Adversarial Role

Begins with the incisive understanding that economic stability is the bedrock upon which a nation stands firm. An adversary keen on undermining this stability need not look further than the fiscal policies that govern the nation's heartbeats: its treasury, its trade, and its trust in the currency. It's in this facet that foes can wage a silent but deadly war, where the weapons are debt, deficits, and the deliberate distortion of currency values.

Envisioning such fiscal challenges requires slipping into the shoes of those who would wish to see our economic structures falter. They'd first target confidence, sowing seeds of distrust in financial institutions and federal economic directives. With strategic misinformation campaigns, that first domino could set a cascade in motion, leading to increased skepticism among citizens and investors alike, resulting in market volatility.

The manipulative adversary would understand that fiscal policy is not just a domestic concern but a global game of chess. They would prioritize efforts to disrupt international trade agreements and foster protectionism. A protectionist America, while attractive through a certain lens, would make the nation vulnerable to shortages, price hikes, and retaliatory measures from global trade partners.

Taxation strategies are another arena ripe for exploitation. The adversary would agitate for both extremes: either for tax policies so lenient they drain essential public services of their lifeblood or so onerous they stifle growth and innovation. They know that either extreme signals an imbalanced fiscal approach, leading to long-term economic ailments.

Debt accumulation is akin to building a house on a foundation of sand; it is the Achilles' heel that an adversary would vigorously attack. With a nation's debt increasing, our hypothetical adversaries could catalyze a crisis of confidence in national bonds, deterring global investment, and potentially triggering a cataclysmic fall in the value of the dollar.

The tactic of exploiting currency manipulation is not lost upon our imagined adversaries. They're aware that if they can influence the dollar's strength against global currencies, they can effectively alter the landscape of international trade, making American exports less competitive while ballooning the cost of imports.

Within the financial sector, an adversarial gaze would turn towards the Federal Reserve, an entity that stands as the guardian of monetary policy. Malign influences could instigate polarized debates over its independence, fostering an atmosphere of uncertainty that could paralyze the decisive action needed to steer a nation through economic turbulence.

The infrastructure upon which an economy thrives—its roads, bridges, and networks—could also come under the adversarial spotlight. The strategy would be to emphasize over or under-investment, either draining the treasury through disproportionate spending or allowing infrastructure to decay, eroding the arteries of commerce and industry.

Let's not underestimate the pragmatism of adversaries in exploiting fiscal policy for social engineering. By amplifying the fractures within society over welfare and entitlement reforms, adversaries can deepen societal rifts, diverting attention from common goals and collective fiscal responsibility.

Social Security—a beloved program seen as a promise to the nation's elderly—would likewise be on the adversary's radar. They'd propagate alarmist narratives about its sustainability to induce a state of intergenerational mistrust and conflict, undermining the societal consensus that bolsters such social programs.

Even the nation's approach to education funding would be fair game. An adversarial critic would argue for severe cuts under the guise of fiscal responsibility or, conversely, for unchecked spending. Both extremes serve the untoward purpose of destabilizing an essential pillar of economic sustainability—investment in human capital.

Furthermore, our fiscal adversary would not overlook healthcare, an industry that represents a significant portion of the GDP. By instigating heated debates over healthcare access and insurance, they can create a fog of war that obscures the need for thoughtful reform and fiscal foresight.

In the realm of national defense spending, such an adversary would strive to unbalance the scales. They'd push for either exorbitant spending to strain the nation's fiscal stability or advocate for drastic cuts that would weaken national security—each move calculated to induce strategic vulnerability.

Lastly, America's adversaries would be poised to manipulate the complex interplay between environmental policy and fiscal responsibility. They understand that extreme positions on either side can cause fiscal upheaval, whether through unsustainable environmental initiatives or negligent practices that lead to costly long-term consequences.

Understanding the adversarial approach to America's fiscal challenges isn't merely an exercise in abstract thought; it's a vital chess move in the game of national security and prosperity. It's through this lens that we can better anticipate and negate the strategies of those who would seek to destabilize the nation's fiscal foundations and, by extension, its global standing and influence.

Defending American Prosperity and Innovation

Stands as a formidable shield raised against the tide of challenges besieging our nation's economic structure and inventive spirit. The vigor and resilience of American prosperity rest not just on mere chance or historical momentum but on a deliberate culture of innovation, nurtured by a rich fabric of freedom and competitive dynamism. At the heart of American prosperity lies a distinct respect for the entrepreneur, the thinker, the risk-taker—each playing a role in an economic drama that has lifted millions out of poverty and into the realms of opportunity.

To safeguard this prosperity, we must acknowledge the multitudinous external forces posed against us. International competitors, armed with strategies to dethrone America's preeminent position in global markets, continue to offer the sternest test of our capacity to innovate and adapt. Thus, defending our prosperity is much more than mere economic policy—it is a strategic imperative that resonates with the very essence of national security.

Innovation, the fountain from which American prowess continuously springs forth, faces incessant assault from those who wish to replicate, appropriate, and, at worst, sabotage the engines of our creativity. It is an elemental truth that the strength of the American economy is bound tightly to the scope and quality of its innovations. Consequently, robust protections for intellectual property, fair and equitable patent laws, and incentives for research and development are not mere legislative preferences but bulwarks against the erosion of our competitive edge.

Yet, adversaries are not only found across oceans; they frequent the domestic arena in the form of overregulation, crippling bureaucracy, and a tax code that at times stifles rather than stimulates growth. To dismantle these internal barriers is to free the intrinsic entrepreneurial spirit that is characteristically American and allow it to flourish without undue hindrance.

Fostering a culture of enterprise extends beyond the shores of Silicon Valley; it demands educational reform that lays the groundwork for critical thinking and creativity from the earliest years.

A system that idolizes rote memorization over innovative thinking is one that prepares the path for mediocrity, not greatness. Our mission then becomes clear: to impart knowledge that is as versatile as it is profound, as practical as it is theoretical.

Societal tenets such as a free-market philosophy and the rule of law are indispensable allies in the defense of prosperity. They lend predictability and structure to economic activities, catalyzing a climate where inventiveness can not only germinate but thrive. Indeed, the sanctity of contracts and the swift adjudication of disputes are cornerstones upon which the skyscrapers of our financial districts rest.

Trade policy, an arena rife with contention and negotiation, must double as a strategic tool through which our standards for labor, environmental protection, and innovation infuse into the global arena, setting benchmarks that uphold our values and economic interests alike. The art of negotiation is such that it should project our economic philosophy as much as it protects our markets.

Simultaneously, the menace of theft and subterfuge cannot be overstated. Corporate espionage and cyber piracy are modern-day pirates pillaging the vaults of our ingenuity. Vigilance and resilience in cybersecurity represent not a choice but an obligation to preserve the integrity of our industries and the privacy of our citizens. In this digital age, cybersecurity is the new frontier of defense—a frontline that is as invisible as it is integral.

The promotion of start-ups and small businesses through venture capital and entrepreneurial support programs inject fresh blood into the arteries of our economy. These initiatives mirror the American Dream's core promise, offering a beacon of hope that talent coupled with hard work and ingenuity will receive its due reward, irrespective of one's starting point in life.

Energy independence, too, plays a pivotal role in fortifying our nation's economy. Advances in technology have opened avenues for extracting and harnessing resources in a manner that was inconceivable mere decades ago. A strategic approach to energy policy that champions sustainability alongside self-sufficiency empowers our nation to steer clear of the turbulent waters of geopolitical oil squabbles.

Infrastructure, though often overshadowed by more glamorous aspects of the economy, forms the literal foundation upon which commerce and innovation travel. Investment in robust physical and digital infrastructure is an investment in the arteries of activity that keep American business pulsing and competitive on a global scale. It is the stage upon which the theater of American innovation performs.

Building a synergy between private industry and public researchers presents another axis along which innovation can be amplified. When the laboratory breakthroughs of public academia are translated into commercially viable products and services through private enterprise, the entire nation reaps the windfall. This symbiotic relationship strengthens a marketplace of ideas that stands second to none.

In the international realm, the maintenance of strong and fair trade agreements serves not only to protect our domestic industries but also to propel our technological dominance. Through these agreements, we can ensure that international competitors play by the rules that keep competition healthy and innovation-driven economies, such as ours, thriving.

And yet, amidst these tactical considerations, it is perhaps the spirit of the American people that is the most enduring defender of our prosperity and innovation. It is a spirit characterized by boldness, imagination, and an unyielding belief in the possibility of a better tomorrow. This enduring trait has been, and will continue to be, the primary architect of our successes and the guardian against stagnation.

As we charter our course into uncertain and rapidly evolving economic waters, we do so with the firm conviction that the essence of American prosperity and innovation—once defended, encouraged, and allowed to reach its potential—will herald an era of progress and prosperity that is not only sustainable but expands the realm of the possible. It is then up to each guardian of this legacy, from policymakers to industrial leaders, from educators to entrepreneurs, to wage this great defense—a defense not only of an economy or an idea but of an identity that is uniquely and proudly American.

Chapter 9:
Cyber Frontiers: America's Virtual Battlegrounds

Stepping across the precipice of physical borders into the expanse that is our nation's digital realm, Chapter 9 unveils the emergent theater of conflict in the cyber domain. As the digital landscape unfolds as an arena laden with both peril and potential, this section unravels the intricate web of cyber threats that shadow America's continued push for globalization and technological supremacy. We stand at a juncture where virtual defense is as paramount as that over land, air, and sea. Grasping the extent of digital incursions by state and non-state actors becomes not just a matter of intellectual discourse, but a clarion call for action to fortify the bedrock of our national cyber strategies. It isn't merely hypothetical; our enemies tirelessly engineer cyber attacks aimed to undermine our electoral integrity, pilfer sensitive information and sow discord within our society. Thus, we delve into the virtual battlegrounds that epitomize this modern frontier, emboldening our resolve to stay vigilant and build resilient infrastructures that secure the American way of life against adversaries who lurk behind screens and keyboards, plotting in the shadows.

Assessing Cyber Threats from an Adversarial Position

Pertains directly to the digital realm, a domain as crucial to our nation's security as our land, sea, and air. When we talk about assessing these threats, we're delving deep into the psyche of our adversaries, trying to understand their motives, capabilities, and opportunities for exploitation. This is not just about knowing your enemy; it is about predicting their moves and staying two steps ahead.

From the vantage point of those who would do us harm, cyber warfare is a cost-effective, asymmetrical tool that can be wielded to great effect. Our digitally interconnected world presents opportunities at every turn for those who know where to look and how to exploit the seams in our defenses. The goal for these adversaries is to undermine our national security, steal our intellectual property, and sow discord among our ranks.

To truly assess these threats, one must first accept a cold truth: our systems, as advanced as they are, carry inherent vulnerabilities. Any system made by humans can be undone by humans. This acknowledgment is not defeatism; it's a starting point for robust defense. It is the cornerstone of any strategy meant to protect our digital frontiers from foreign intrusion and domestic subversion.

In understanding the cyber attacker's mindset, we must consider their objectives. For some, it's a matter of national strategy, a way to weaken a geopolitical rival without ever firing a shot. For others, it's economic gain, be it through ransomware, theft of intellectual property, or manipulation of financial systems. And for yet others, it's ideological, seeking to disrupt and influence democratic processes and societal cohesion.

Consideration of the 'kill chain' model, a term borrowed from military doctrine, provides a structured framework for understanding how an adversary might plan and execute a cyber attack. Recognizing each phase—reconnaissance, weaponization, delivery, exploitation, installation, command and control, and action—allows defenders to anticipate and disrupt these actions at every step.

Toolkits and methods of cyber adversaries are constantly evolving, as are their targets. Critical infrastructure, an all-too-tempting target, if compromised, could lead to catastrophic consequences. Disrupting or controlling utilities such as power, water, or transportation systems, could not only create immediate chaos but also shake public confidence in government's ability to safeguard its citizenry.

Intelligence-gathering is central to countering cyber threats. One must actively monitor forums, chat rooms, and marketplaces in the dark web—those portions of the internet where anonymity reigns and illicit activities flourish. This is where threats germinate and often where they are first signaled. Understanding the adversary's language and codes can provide an early warning to impending attacks.

Social engineering remains a preferred technique for many cyber adversaries due to its reliance on human error rather than technological prowess—tricking individuals into breaking standard security procedures. In protecting against these threats, therefore, the focus must not just be on hardware and software. It's equally essential to foster a culture of cybersecurity awareness and vigilance within organizations.

Another tactic from the adversary's playbook is exploiting the divide between public and private sectors when it comes to cybersecurity. Many of our critical systems are owned and operated by private entities, which may not have the same level of resources or information as government agencies to defend against sophisticated threats. Bridging this gap is crucial for a holistic defense.

When assessing these threats, we must also keep in mind that our adversaries are learning from our responses. They adapt to our defenses and evolve their strategies accordingly. It's a game of cat and mouse—a continuous cycle of action and reaction. Cybersecurity is a dynamic field, and complacency can lead to disaster. Vigilance is not just a responsibility; it's a necessity.

Moreover, the cyber realm offers our adversaries plausible deniability. Attack attribution in cyberspace is complex and often convoluted, giving attackers the cover they need to operate with impunity. This ambiguity can hamper diplomatic responses and allows state and non-state actors to engage in cyber operations without overt repercussions.

It also becomes clear that the cyber domain is a leveling field. Small nations and non-state actors can have a disproportionate impact, challenging the conventional tenets of power and influence. For those seeking to assess cyber threats from an adversarial position, understanding this dynamic is crucial. Asymmetry can work in both ways, and innovative defensive strategies can also level the playing field against more resourceful adversaries.

To stay ahead, it is imperative to conduct regular penetration testing and red team exercises. These simulations of an adversary's attack on our own systems serve as a stress test for our cyber defenses, uncovering unknown vulnerabilities and providing invaluable insights into our security posture. It's an adversarial analysis executed to benefit our own protection.

When assessing cyber threats, one must also explore the secondary and tertiary consequences of an adversary's actions. For instance, the fallout of a data breach extends beyond the immediate loss of information—it can affect the credibility of institutions, diminish public trust, and lead to broader societal and political repercussions.

Ultimately, the art of assessing cyber threats from an adversarial position is about more than just understanding the technology. It's about grasping the broader context in which these threats occur—geopolitical, economic, and social—and having a nuanced appreciation of the human element at play. Knowing how and why an adversary might strike is our best defense in guarding the digital gateways to our nation's future.

Strengthening National Cyber Strategies

In the realm of national defense, the cyber dimension has become just as critical as land, sea, air, and space. Our adversaries, both state and rogue entities, don't slumber; they relentlessly probe and penetrate virtual barriers, aiming to compromise our security, pilfer our intellectual properties, and subvert our democratic processes. As such, it's incumbent upon us to fortify our cyber strategies with the same vigor we apply to tangible battlefronts. In this vein, we delve into strengthening national cyber strategies.

Initiating the conversation with a robust national cybersecurity framework is imperative. This framework serves as the backbone for protecting critical infrastructures, governmental agencies, and private sector entities integral to our country's functioning and security. By building upon a set of established standards, best practices, and guidelines, we can foster a collaborative environment where the sharing of threat intelligence isn't just welcomed but expected.

Investment in research and development must be steadfast and unwavering. The digital battlefield evolves with dizzying speed, and staying ahead requires a commitment to innovation and the continual updating of our cyber arsenal. Public-private partnerships can be particularly effective here, marrying governmental foresight with the creativity and agility of the tech sector.

Education and workforce development are crucial in this endeavor. Developing a pipeline of skilled cybersecurity professionals is a strategic imperative that cannot be overlooked. Initiatives to stimulate interest in STEM fields, combined with educational pathways that lead to careers in cybersecurity, are vital to maintaining a robust defense against cyber threats.

Policies that encourage and even mandate cyber hygiene can serve as a bulwark against cyber attacks. Individual users often represent the weakest link in the security chain, and through comprehensive education campaigns, we can cultivate a more secure digital culture. We need to impart the importance of basic practices such as using strong passwords, recognizing phishing attempts, and keeping software up to date.

Diplomacy plays a role, too. Crafting international standards and norms for cyber conduct, and rallying allies to commit to these norms, lays the groundwork for a united front against global cyber threats. It also provides a framework for accountability, allowing nations to collectively condemn and sanction entities that perpetrate cyber warfare.

Our legal systems must adapt to the virtual domain seeking justice and deterrence against cybercriminals. Strengthening legislation to prosecute cybercrimes effectively and establishing international legal cooperation are necessary to chase down perpetrators, even across borders. We must develop extradition agreements and mutual legal assistance treaties that account for the borderless nature of cyber warfare.

Interagency coordination within the federal government elevates our cyber readiness. Siloed efforts lead to gaps that adversaries can exploit. A unified, whole-of-government approach to cybersecurity, in which information and resources flow freely amongst agencies with cyber responsibility such as the Department of Homeland Security, FBI, and NSA, serves to present a formidable defense.

Exercising and simulating cyberattacks are key. Regularly scheduled cyber exercises enable us to test the resilience of our systems and our ability to respond rapidly to cyber incidents. These exercises help to reveal vulnerabilities and prepare our cyber task forces for the eventuality of a real-world attack.

Adapting cyber strategies to emerging technologies ensures longevity and relevance. Technologies such as quantum computing and artificial intelligence promise to revolutionize the cyber landscape. We must work to understand these technologies' potential impacts on security and integrate them into our defense strategies accordingly.

We must also recognise the potential of cyber strategies to empower non-state actors. With the democratization of cyber tools, small groups can wield disproportionate power. Our strategies must anticipate and mitigate this threat, ensuring that measures are in place to counteract the rise of cyber-enabled extremism and terrorism.

Supply chain security is a crucial aspect of cybersecurity. We must scrutinise and secure the supply chains that underpin our critical infrastructures and military systems. This includes close monitoring of vendors and developing stringent cybersecurity requirements for suppliers at all levels.

Beyond defense, we need to explore the offensive capabilities within the cyber domain. Just as deterrence is a principle of physical warfare, the ability to launch cyber counterattacks is a necessary component of a comprehensive national cyber strategy. These offensive capabilities can serve to dissuade adversaries from undertaking cyber aggression against us in the first place.

Public awareness and engagement are vital in reinforcing national cyber strategies. A well-informed populace is less likely to fall prey to cyber manipulation and can serve as an additional layer of observation and deterrence. Efforts to keep the public apprised of the latest cyber threats and protective measures cultivate a culture of resilience.

Finally, review and revision of cyber strategies must be continual. Cyber threats are fluid and ever-changing, and so too must be our strategies to combat them. Regular evaluation of the effectiveness of our cyber strategies allows us to refine and adapt them to the shifting digital landscape. It helps ensure that we are not left floundering in the wake of the next major cyber assault, but rather, that we emerge stronger and more prepared than ever before.

Through these comprehensive and sustained efforts, we can aim to secure not just our digital infrastructures but also the very values and systems that define our society. The war in cyberspace is a modern reality — one that demands resourcefulness, resolve, and a forward-looking vision. Our national cyber strategies are the bulwarks of freedom's future, and in strengthening them, we safeguard our nation's prosperity, security, and democratic way of life.

Chapter 10:
The Global Chessboard: Playing for High Stakes

In a world where geopolitical dynamics constantly shift beneath our feet, understanding the high-stakes game on the global chessboard isn't just important—it's imperative for national survival. Dissecting the motives and maneuvers of global adversaries requires insight that pierces through the fog of international rhetoric. It's here we analyze how nations pull the strings in a complex theatre of power, planting seeds of influence and fostering alliances that can either flourish into partnerships or decay into hostilities. As we project American strength and influence, we must balance assertiveness with diplomacy, ensuring we're equipped to tackle brewing storms on the international horizon. By adapting our strategies to counterweight the ambitions of those who may wish to tilt the balance of global power, we maintain the foresight to not only react to worldwide events but also to shape them. This intricate dance of global influence doesn't just yield immediate outcomes; it also plants the seeds for a future wherein our nation's values can stand firm in the face of shifting allegiances and emerging challenges.

Behind Enemy Lines: Insight into Global Adversaries

It's an enduring truth that to safeguard a nation, one must develop a keen understanding of potential foes. Cast your gaze across our world's vast geopolitical theater, and the contours of confrontation are drawn sharp. From flexing economic muscles to cyber sabotage, the great powers navigate a complex web of competition and challenge.

At the heart of this intricate dance lie our global adversaries—who are they, what drives them, and how do we grapple with the rising tide of their ambitions? These rivals range widely in form and focus: nation-states seeking to challenge the existing world order, rogue regimes threatening international stability with nuclear ambitions, and non-state actors orchestrating terror and disruption.

Diving deep into the psyche of these adversaries requires a meticulous approach—an approach that doesn't merely skim the surface of their military might, but unravels the underlying motives propelling their agendas forward. Their histories, cultures, and grievances lay the groundwork. They inform strategy, ambition, and the distillation of ideology into action.

In the realm of superpower dynamics, consider the enduring riddle of containment versus engagement. There's a need to decipher the strategic calculus that drives nations like China and Russia. China, with its Belt and Road Initiative, seeks to weave a narrative of economic indispensability, while Russia, through its myriad geopolitical maneuvers, aims to resurrect an aura of superpower influence reminiscent of its Cold War-era stature.

Let's not overlook the Middle Eastern canvass, embroiled in its complicated blend of ethnic strife and regional hegemonies. Here lies Iran, with its nuclear aspirations and support for proxy warriors, presenting a perpetual puzzle for policymakers aiming to stabilize an already volatile region. Meanwhile, North Korea continues its high-stakes brinkmanship, oscillating between diplomatic engagement and defiant missile tests.

Today's landscape is further complicated by the emergence of hybrid and asymmetric warfare, with foes operating in the shadows, employing cyberattacks, disinformation campaigns, and other subversive tactics. We're not just defending against armies but also fighting to preserve the integrity of our institutions and the cohesion of our societies against these stealth raids.

The shifting sands of international alliances add another layer of complexity. Allies today could be pressured or circumstances manipulated, such that they become adversaries tomorrow. The United States must proactively foster relationships that reinforce democratic ideals and mutual interests while recognizing the fluid nature of global alliances.

Delving into economic leverage, we see adversaries weaponizing trade, exploiting the interconnectedness that globalization brings forth. They bend international organizations to their will, flouting norms to gain competitive edges in technology, resources, and market dominance. There's a fine line between competitive economics and outright economic warfare—a line that our adversaries are all too willing to blur.

Look at the exhaustion of perpetual conflict zones, where warlords and terror groups exploit power vacuums. These actors don't adhere to the Geneva Conventions or any semblance of international law. Instead, they rely on terror, brutality, and the erosion of civil society to maintain their foothold. Their narratives are laced with propaganda, geared to sow dissent and instability.

In understanding the adversary's mind, one cannot discount the role of ideology as a driving force. Whether it's radical extremism or the strategic dissemination of authoritarian doctrines, these beliefs permeate borders and influence populations, becoming a pivotal factor in the game of international relations.

No longer can we ignore the digital realm as a primary domain of confrontation. Cyber intrusions into critical infrastructure, electoral interference, and information warfare are the new frontline. Our adversaries recruit legions of hackers, infiltrating the unseen veins of society, disrupting systems, and commandeering narratives to their advantage.

But awareness alone is not the safeguard against these threats. The United States must bolster its resilience, from tightening cybersecurity and safeguarding critical networks, to investing in counterintelligence capabilities that can unmask and thwart covert operations.

To effectively navigate the treacherous waters of global politics, it is crucial to exercise strategic restraint and calculated response. Preemptive aggression can sometimes be the spark that ignites full-scale conflict. Instead, the United States must harness the power of diplomacy, forging partnerships, and championing international norms to counteract adversarial advances.

Despite their prowess or persistence, these global adversaries also grapple with internal challenges—economic woes, demographic shifts, and domestic unrest. It is within these fissures that opportunities for the U.S. to subtly influence and mitigate adversarial threats may arise. A multi-faceted strategy that applies pressure and extends the olive branch where beneficial could shift the balance in favor of global stability.

Concluding this analytical expedition behind enemy lines, we return fortified with insights that demand action. Visionary leadership stands at the vanguard, crafting strategies that not only respond to immediate threats but also anticipate the long game. For it's in the understanding of adversaries—not just their machinations, but their very psyche—that a nation can navigate the uncertain tides of global relations and emerge steadfast, resilient, and ever vigilant.

Projecting American Strength and Influence

Projecting American Strength and Influence has been at the forefront of the United States' international strategy for decades. The projection of this power is not merely through military might, but through an entwined web of diplomatic ties, cultural influence, and economic prowess. As we navigate through this global chessboard, we must understand the nuanced ways in which America asserts its place as a world leader.

To begin with, one of the core methods for America to project its strength is through its network of alliances. Alliances such as NATO and partnerships with countries like Japan and South Korea help ensure that America's global reach is backed by a consensus of shared values and mutual defense agreements. By upholding these bonds, America sends a clear message of unity and prepared facilitation for collective security.

Moreover, economic sanctions have become a pivotal tool in the arsenal of American foreign policy. By controlling access to the world's largest economy, the United States can exert significant pressure on nations that go against international norms. Whether it's sanctions on rogue nations or tariffs strategically placed to protect national industries, the economy is as much a part of America's sphere of influence as its military is.

Further cementing its influence, America's cultural output remains unmatched. Hollywood, Silicon Valley, and the music industry, among others, offer the soft power that shapes global tastes, opinions, and desires. This cultural exportation not only generates economic wealth but also serves to propagate the American way of life, subtly reinforcing its values on the world stage.

However, the strategic positioning of overseas military bases is undoubtedly a significant aspect of American influence. These bases enable rapid response to global crises and demonstrate an unwavering commitment to the defense of American interests and those of its allies. The ubiquity of American military presence has long been perceived as a stabilizing factor in volatile regions.

Diplomacy, too, serves as a corner-stone in spreading American sway. The Department of State, through skilled diplomacy, negotiates treaties, provides humanitarian aid, and embodies the nation's commitment to global cooperation. Strategic foreign aid can create dependable allies and foster an image of goodwill, an invaluable asset in geopolitics.

Yet the projection of American influence can be fraught with tensions. The delicate balance between defending national interests and upholding international law is a continual diplomatic tightrope walk. Strikes with precision-guided munitions and clandestine operations by special forces are approved, only when absolutely necessary, to neutralize threats and display resolve while striving to preserve the normative global order.

Information warfare is also a domain where America must continually assert its dominance. Ensuring the integrity and security of communication systems against misinformation campaigns is pivotal. By promoting an open, reliable flow of information, America strengthens its narrative and diminishes the impact of adversarial propaganda.

Educational exchange programs, such as the Fulbright Scholarship, represent another subtle, yet powerful aspect of spreading influence. These opportunities plant the seeds of American perspectives among the global future elite, thus fostering a worldwide network that often holds favorable views towards the United States on their return to their home countries.

The axis of American strength also revolves around scientific research and development. By maintaining a leadership role in cutting-edge innovations, the United States influences global standards and practices across numerous industries. This leadership not only dictates market trends but also ensures that American interests shape future technological landscapes.

However, projecting strength is not just about displaying muscles; it's about demonstrating resilience. Whether it's recovering from economic recession, dealing with social upheaval, or managing natural disasters, the world watches how America handles adversity. Effective domestic policy responses not only strengthen national unity but also reassure international observers of American stability and competence.

Trade agreements, like NAFTA and its successor USMCA, extend American influence into the economic structures of neighboring countries, and by extension, the world. These instruments of policy craft a milieu of economic interdependence wherein America often assures a central role, serving as the linchpin to major trade blocs and shaping global trade policies to its advantage.

In pursuit of global peace and security, America's commitment to arms control and non-proliferation efforts demonstrate the nation's dedication to responsibility on the world stage. By leading by example in reducing stockpiles and securing materials, America fortifies its moral standing and ethical authority in international discourse.

Yet, maintaining this projection of strength requires constant vigilance. The United States must not only respond to immediate crises but also anticipate future challenges through a robust and far-sighted foreign policy. It's about being proactive, not reactive, and setting a global agenda that aligns with American principles and safeguards its interests.

As we project American strength and influence across the globe, it's imperative to remember that such power should be wielded with discernment and grace. A nuanced blend of strength and diplomacy is required to champion the nation's interests in harmony with its values - for influence is most enduring when it is embraced rather than imposed.

In conclusion, the United States continues to stand as a beacon of liberty, innovation, and leadership on the world stage. Projecting strength and influence is about much more than show of force; it is about inspiring partnerships, fostering growth, and posit a transformative example. As we move forward, it is this combination of might, mind, and moral clarity that will define America's role in the world and ensure that its influence remains as beneficial as it is profound.

Chapter 11:
Medical Battlefield: Navigating
Pandemic Politics

Emerging from the global chessboard's complex maze, our focus shifts to a more insidious adversary that transcends borders and political affiliations: disease. Chapter 11 delves into the labyrinth of pandemic politics where ideology and public health are often at odds. The art of navigation through this medical battlefield demands more than scientific acumen; it requires a piercing analysis of the socio-political landscape, which can mean the difference between containment and catastrophe. We unravel the strategic interplay between pathogens and politics, dissecting how decision-makers mold responses that echo across freedoms and economies. It's an unflinching examination of resilience amidst biological threats, spotlighting the relentless pursuit to safeguard our nation's health without compromising the foundational liberties that give it life.

Pathogen Pathways: The Health Security Dilemma

In the quest to navigate the labyrinth of national security, one cannot overlook the intricate web of pathogen pathways. These invisible threats, unbeknownst to the naked eye, weave themselves into the fabrics of society, igniting a health security dilemma of colossal proportions. The conversation around biological hazards is not simply a matter of science fiction, it is a contemporary geopolitical reality. The scope of this analysis hinges on the profound understanding that the health of a nation extends beyond its physical borders.

In confronting the health security dilemma, it becomes imperative to grasp the vast and complex networks these pathogens traverse. From the natural to the anthropogenic, the origins are as varied as their methods of dissemination. Their vectors know no boundaries, transcending oceans and piercing through the defenses of even the most prepared nations. This invisible enemy necessitates a vanguard strategy, one that is as agile and adaptive as the pathogens themselves.

The unforgiving nature of biological pathogens in the modern era poses a challenge that is unique to our time. With the advent of globalization, the movement of people and goods creates an interconnected domain where pathogens hitch rides, crossing from one continent to another with ease. The acceleration of travel and trade has shrunk the world, enhancing the potential for rapid spread and escalation of disease outbreaks.

Undeniably, the realm of public health is a battlefield of its own. The adversary is elusive, and the stakes are high, as the well-being of millions hangs in the balance. The concept of biosecurity must evolve to meet the pressing demands of this century, entailing not just scientific acumen but also political will and social resilience. It is a mantle that governments, institutions, and individuals must collectively shoulder.

To address this health security dilemma, it is critical to cultivate strategic foresight. Preparedness plans and surveillance systems need to be as dynamic as the biological threats we face. History has taught us that it is not a question of if, but when the next pathogen will emerge. And so, nations must develop robust frameworks for rapid response, integrating the efforts of health agencies, law enforcement, and policymakers.

Moreover, health security is an issue of equitable importance. Pathogen pathways do not discriminate, affecting rich and poor alike, yet the capacity to respond is invariably stratified by socioeconomic factors. Herein lies a moral imperative; to build capacities in every corner of the globe. International cooperation is indispensable in this fight, for the outbreak of disease anywhere is a threat to health everywhere.

One cannot separate the debate on health security from the fervor of political discourse. Responses to health crises often become entangled with political ideologies, leading to polarized reactions over containment strategies, resource allocation, and civil liberties. The narrative constructed around an outbreak can either unify or divide, empower or paralyze a nation.

Transparency and communication play pivotal roles in the management of health crises. During such events, information becomes as potent as any vaccine or treatment. Misinformation and fear are companions of the pathogen, hindering response efforts, and cultivating distrust. Clear, consistent, and fact-based messaging from leadership and health authorities is paramount to foster public compliance and maintain social order.

As we scan the horizon for emergent threats, the integration of technology in tracking and combating pathogens becomes a beacon of hope. The speed at which genetic sequencing and data analytics have advanced is astonishing. These technological frontiers offer the promise of faster outbreak detection, personalized medicine, and targeted interventions, potentially curtailing the pathways through which pathogens spread.

Yet, on the flip side of this coin lies the dark specter of bioterrorism. The very innovations that could save us can also be turned against us. The manipulation of biological agents for nefarious purposes is a grim reality, one that requires vigilance and robust countermeasures. This dual-use nature of biotechnology is a paradox that we must navigate with caution, ensuring advancements in the field do not inadvertently open new avenues for attack.

The health security dilemma underscores the interdependency of global health and national security. A nation's resilience to biological threats is not solely characterized by its scientific capabilities but also by the strength of its social fabric. Public trust, community engagement, and a culture of preparedness are the underpinnings of a successful defense against pathogen pathways.

As we iterate on strategies to mitigate the health security risks, we must recognize that it is not enough to build walls or close off borders. The nature of these threats requires a more profound introspection. It calls for a reassessment of healthcare systems, a bolstering of international alliances, and a reinvigoration of community-level health awareness.

In this relentless pursuit to secure the health of a nation, we are reminded of our shared humanity. The voice of reason must rise above the din of fear, guiding us toward thoughtful, collective action. For in the grander scheme, the pathogen pathways do not lead to despair but to a greater understanding of the interconnectedness and mutual vulnerabilities we face in our global village.

We stand at a crossroads where science, policy, and ethics converge. The health security dilemma compels us to reimagine a world that is better prepared, more responsive, and eternally vigilant. In this ongoing battle against the microbial adversary, it is innovation, foresight, and unity that will shepherd us through. The path forward may be fraught with uncertainty, but with concerted effort and shared purpose, we hold the keys to safeguarding our future.

The exploration of this health security dilemma does not signify an end but a beginning. As we turn the page to understand the critique of political responses to public health crises, we carry with us the knowledge that the realm of pathogens is a crucible of our times. It is a testament to our capacity for resilience, collaboration, and the indefatigable human spirit that always seeks to persevere, even in the face of the unseen foes that threaten to unravel our societal fabric.

Critique of Political Responses to Public Health Crises –

We have found ourselves at a critical juncture where the fusion of politics and public health creates a battleground thick with ideology and rhetoric. It is paramount for citizens to sift through the cacophony of political discourse to find the truth behind how public health crises are managed and manipulated by those in power.

Throughout history, governments have had to respond to a myriad of health emergencies, some of which have reshaped societies and altered the course of history. Yet, as we dissect the political responses to these crises, questions arise concerning the prioritization of public welfare against the backdrop of political gain.

In dealing with a public health crisis, any government's initial response is a telltale sign of its preparedness and foresight. Nevertheless, too often we witness a lack of alacrity, where the sluggish recognition of an emerging health threat translates into exacerbated outcomes. The missteps become apparent only in hindsight, provoking inquiries about the missing sense of urgency.

The complexity of a public health crisis often unmasks a government's tendency to politicize the event. Whether by downplaying risks to avoid panic or economic downturns or by magnifying threats to consolidate power, the political spin impacts public perception and trust. The implications of such actions have far-reaching consequences on compliance with public health measures and, ultimately, on the efficacy of disease containment.

Transparency—or the lack thereof—is the cornerstone of how political responses are judged when managing a health crisis. Information is key, and the dissemination of accurate data is non-negotiable. Yet we observe that transparency can suffer at the altar of political expediency, where the control of information becomes a strategic game rather than a public right.

While battling a health crisis, the rhetoric employed by governmental authorities can either unify or polarize a population. When leaders utilize the crisis to blame, scapegoat, or otherwise divert attention from pressing issues, it creates divisiveness that can hinder a collective response and slow healing and recovery efforts.

Financial allocations and budgetary support for public health initiatives are always a contentious topic. Funding, often politicized, can determine the speed and thoroughness of a crisis response. Observing which programs are financed and which are not reveals the underlying priorities and sometimes the uncomfortable truth that public health can play second fiddle to other interests.

Collaboration between different levels of government and with international bodies plays a crucial role in managing a health crisis. When politics interfere with establishing or maintaining these relationships, the resulting silos and protectionism can dramatically stifle a comprehensive approach to public health emergencies.

Strategic communication during a public health crisis is not only about what is said but also about how it is said. We notice time and again that fear tactics and alarmist messaging can shape public behavior in unpredictable ways, often to the detriment of sound public health policy.

The role of scientific expertise has become politicized, with polarized debates overshadowing the merit of evidence-based decisions. When science is subjugated to political will or ideology, the outcomes can be devastating, leading to loss of life that could have been mitigated with an apolitical approach to scientific facts.

Long-term strategy for public health resilience is often neglected due to political short-termism. Investment in robust health infrastructure, proactive disease surveillance, and research is usually underserved, as it may not culminate in immediate political dividends. Yet, these are the vital cogs in the wheel of effective public health crisis management.

Regulatory responses in the heat of a health crisis are another prism through which political maneuvering can be scrutinized. Sometimes, regulations are enforced with heavy-handedness or without reasonable flexibility, causing more harm than good and demonstrating a lack of nuance and understanding from political figures.

Political accountability in the aftermath of a public health emergency is frequently elusive. Ensuring that lessons are learned and can better inform future responses seems secondary to the rush for vindication and the shifting of blame, an attitude that is counterproductive to growth and preparation for future challenges.

The integrity of public health messaging during a crisis must be safeguarded against political interference. Communication strategies driven by political objectives compromise the sanctity of the message and the health of the populace. Here, the role of independent media and fact-checking becomes a vital counterbalance to potential misinformation.

In conclusion, to navigate the treacherous waters of a public health crisis, the political responses must be held to the highest scrutiny. A vigilant populace that demands transparency, accountability, and a science-based approach is the fulcrum of resilience in the face of such crises. As we come to terms with the reality that health emergencies will recur, our preparedness and the integrity of our political systems will consistently be tested. It is in our collective hands to ensure that political responses serve the public good, emerging from these crises stronger, more united, and more informed than before.

Chapter 12:
Educational Crossfire: Shaping
the Next Generation

As we pivot from the Medical Battlefield's analysis, we venture into the potent arena of education, where the hearts and minds of future citizens are forged amidst ongoing ideological skirmishes. In this chapter, we delve into the dynamic discourse surrounding educational system reform, where the champions of academic freedom wrestle with the custodians of traditional pedagogy. The future of our nation hinges on the narratives we embed within the classroom walls; thus, examining the crafting of curricula becomes much more than a mere academic debate—it's a profound responsibility vested upon us. When we consider the preservation of American history and ideals in academia, we're not just preserving facts for posterity; we're inspiring the next generation to build upon a bedrock of informed patriotism. This chapter stakes its claim on the very crux of our educational policy, setting the lens through which upcoming stewards will perceive their roles in this great experiment of democracy.

Curricula and Controversy: Analyzing Educational Policies

The landscape of the American educational system is as dynamic and contentious as ever. Policies stand at the crossroads of ideological battles, inciting heated debates that resonate far beyond the confines of classrooms and lecture halls. As our journey through the nation's current adversarial climate continues, let's turn our analytical gaze to the very bedrock that shapes the minds of future generations: the curricula they are exposed to and the controversies they incite.

The fault lines in educational policy debates are not merely over the intricacies of pedagogy or the finer points of child development; they touch upon the very core of what society deems valuable knowledge. Central to these debates is a question of influence: who has the right to decide what is taught to rising young minds? This is not simply an academic query, but a question loaded with socio-political implications, one that intertwines with the fabric of democracy and individual freedoms.

Curricula have become contested terrain with stakeholders across the political spectrum wielding the policy-making pen. Triggering controversy can be policies oriented towards inclusion of diverse histories, mandates on standard testing, or alterations to the way American history itself is taught. The issue at hand is not only what narrative is given prominence, but also what narratives are being marginalized or omitted outright from the educational conversation.

For instance, the debate over "Common Core" has grown particularly acute, with concerns about nationalized standards supposedly infringing upon local control. Education is constitutionally delegated to the states, and yet there is an inherent tension here: the need for a coherent, nation-wide education system that prepares students equitably, versus the local community's desire to have its values and perspective reflected within the curricula.

At the heart of these curricular disputes is often a fundamental disagreement about the purpose of education. Is it to create well-rounded citizens prepared to engage civilly in a diverse society? Or is it perhaps to nurture future professionals who will drive economic success? Maybe it's to instill a sense of national pride and historical continuity? The answers may vary greatly depending on whom you ask, and policies will diverge accordingly.

Another aspect fostering controversy within educational policies links directly to how students are assessed. Standardized testing, for example, has been both lauded as a measure of accountability and decried as a reductive and inadequate appraisal of student intelligence and teacher competency. Critics contend that it leads to "teaching to the test" and constraining creative and critical thinking. Conversely, proponents argue it's an essential benchmark for equality and excellence.

The controversy further extends into literature, with battles over banned books and what constitutes appropriate material for various age groups. Some see censorship as a barrier to education, while others see it as a necessary guardrail to protect young minds from premature exposure to certain topics. Policies in this realm encapsulate a struggle over the control of cultural narratives and the dissemination of ideas.

Technology and digitization of classrooms have opened a Pandora's box of promise and peril. One side accentuates the opportunity for expansive learning and accessibility which digital media grants, while the opposing view raises alarm bells over privacy concerns, screen addiction, and the digital divide that exacerbates inequality among students with differing access to these resources. Educational policies must navigate these rocky waters with a keen eye on the potential consequences for various demographics.

The voices clamoring for a say in education policy are many and varied. Businesses seek graduates with skills aligned with industry needs. Parents demand security and moral alignment with familial values. Educators advocate for autonomy and resources to facilitate learning effectively. Policymakers are caught in the whirlwind, often trying to reconcile these conflicting demands with fiscal responsibilities and political pressure.

Amidst these debates, one must consider the legal struggles. Lawsuits on affirmative action and discrimination in college admissions showcase the judiciary's role in shaping educational outcomes. These legal disputes can have wide-ranging implications not just for the individuals involved but for the institutions and policies at large. Policymakers, therefore, operate within a complex web of legal precedents and potential litigation.

And let's not overlook the role of teacher unions, whose power to influence educational policy through collective bargaining and political activism is substantial. These unions can be fierce advocates for educators, but their actions often ignite spirited discussions about the balance of power between teachers' rights, administrative control, and students' best interests.

Ultimately, educational policy is not just a platform for academic planning; it's a battleground for the cultural and ideological soul of the nation. Questions of patriotism, revisionism, and historical interpretation have turned curricula into proxies for broader political goals and narratives. Interpreting American history, for instance, can take on a variety of hues depending on the lens through which it's taught.

And let's remember, education doesn't stop at high school graduation. The realm of higher education is rife with its controversies around funding, freedom of speech, and the role colleges and universities should play in society. The discourse around 'safe spaces', the increasing cost of tuition, and the critique of academia as an 'echo chamber' have pulled higher education policies into the national spotlight, reflecting and amplifying the divides seen in the broader public square.

Educational policies are a quintessential example of the intersection between individual autonomy and societal influence. These policies don't just shape minds; they also sculpt the path of the nation, given that today's students are tomorrow's leaders. As such, to engage in the debate around educational policies isn't merely a matter of pedagogical preference; it's to partake in the crafting of America's future narrative.

With this understanding, let us be both diligent and visionary in our approach to educational policy. Let us not shy away from controversy but instead engage with it productively, aware that our conclusions will echo through the generations. Our dedication to thoughtful analysis and strategic foresight in educational policy can ensure that the intellectual tapestry of our nation remains diverse, robust, and enduringly vibrant.

Preservation of American History and Ideals in Academia

As the battleground of ideas shifts to the academic realm, it's essential we anchor our discussions in the pursuit of truth, not just advocacy. American history and its ideals form the backbone of our nation's identity. They're not merely historical waypoints; they resonate as reminders of our ongoing journey toward a more perfect union. In today's academic environments, safeguarding these narratives is more than a nod to the past; it is an investment in our future.

Understanding the context of our origins, the Founding Fathers' intentions, and the evolving interpretation of their words is a crucial aspect of American education. Historical revisionism is not, as some suggest, a way to correct outdated narratives, but rather a threat to the integrity of our shared story when it skews facts to fit contemporary ideologies.

Within the halls of academia, the debate rages over what version of history we choose to impart to the next generation. While inclusivity of diverse perspectives is paramount for a holistic education, there is a thin line between broadening understanding and distorting the essence of historical truth. American academia has a responsibility to portray the nation's history with accuracy and provide the analytical tools for students to understand the nuances and complexities of our past.

Programs centered on constitutional studies and the founding principles are not only instructive but imperative. Students must grapple with the original texts and the debates that shaped them to truly comprehend the ideals upon which this nation was built. Initiatives to deepen civic understanding and respect for the rule of law should be at the heart of the academic journey.

The unequivocal support for educators who strive to preserve the core American values against the tide of ideological reinterpretation is essential. These professionals often face criticism and opposition, but their role in molding critical, well-informed citizens cannot be overstated. It's vital that these educators are provided with the tools and support necessary to teach with confidence and authority.

One cannot underplay the role of academic institutions in fostering an environment where free expression is not just tolerated but encouraged. Freedom of thought and discourse are cornerstones of our democratic society and should be mirrored in our universities and schools. The suppression of ideas, however controversial, on the pretext of preserving social or political harmony, is a disservice to intellectual growth and a direct assault on the foundations of academic freedom.

Furthermore, there's an emerging narrative to redefine patriotism in education as a blind allegiance, but true patriotism is rooted in understanding the trials, tribulations, and triumphs that have shaped the nation. It's about debating, challenging, and ultimately striving to uphold the values that define the American spirit. Encouraging this form of engaged patriotism in the classroom forges a more knowledgeable and conscientious citizenry.

Academic programs must also focus on the integration of lessons that bring to life the American experience. The story of the United States is multifaceted and includes contributions from all its people. This diverse historical tapestry gives context to the country's achievements and shortcomings, thus fostering a more robust and inclusive sense of national heritage.

The digitization of primary source documents and historical archives has opened new doors for students and scholars alike. With these resources increasingly available, we witness a democratization of information that can potentially enrich American history education. By placing primary materials at the fingertips of curious minds, we foster a direct engagement with the past that textbooks simply cannot replicate.

Interdisciplinary approaches that weave together history, political science, economics, and other social sciences ensure that students understand the interconnectivity of American ideals and the functioning of its institutions. This comprehensive approach not only preserves history but illuminates its relevance in shaping contemporary policy and thought.

Remembering the cost of freedom and the sacrifices made to secure it is not an exercise in nostalgia, but a critical component of educational narratives. Our schools and universities must continually remind students of the pricelessness of their liberties. These are not abstract ideals but practical principles fought for and upheld throughout American history.

Learning from past mistakes is as important as celebrating historic achievements. Acknowledging and critiquing previous failings is an exercise in critical thinking and accountability, fostering a more truthful and profound respect for the progress our nation has made and the distance we have yet to traverse.

Lastly, the fostering of leadership skills through the study of great American figures offers invaluable lessons in character, resolve, and vision. These historical figures weren't infallible, but their contributions and legacies provide practical examples of leadership and service. By studying not only their victories but also their struggles and ethical quandaries, students gain a deeper appreciation for the intricacies of governance and responsibility.

In conclusion, the preservation of American history and ideals in academia is not a static endeavor. It is the dynamic, continuous cultivation of awareness, respect, and application of the foundational principles that have shaped the nation. These ideals should be woven into the very fabric of educational institutions, ensuring that with each new class of students, the torch of American heritage burns ever brighter.

As we move into the penultimate sections of this analytical journey, it becomes increasingly apparent that these educational endeavors are imperative, not just for the individual but for the ongoing narrative of our nation. It's through informed, respectful, and proactive academia that we pique the minds that will soon guide us, ensuring the baton of our collective memory and democratic ethos is passed on, untarnished, to the leaders of tomorrow.

Chapter 13:
Embracing the Analytical Vanguard

The steadfast journey through the corridors of our nation's most intricate issues demands an analytical vanguard, a frontline of thinkers who take the analytical approach to every thunderous debate and silent struggle that forms the vibrant tapestry that is America. As such, we stand at the confluence of history and future, tradition and innovation, challenges and triumphs. Our analytical journey has shown us that no corner of our society is without the need for deep analysis and a robust, fact-based dialogue.

Compelled by the spirit of American resolve, we have decoded adversarial thinking in political arenas and prepped ourselves for unforeseen events with strategic foresight. These essences of preparedness lace our thoughts, strengthening the fabric of our convictions. It is paramount that we carry these virtues forward, embracing the analytical vanguard as both shield and compass.

Yet, adoption is only the beginning. Enacting change is rooted in understanding, and so, our comprehension of the immigration debate benefits from an analytical lens, parsing political rhetoric while addressing policy with grounded reality. Here we see the power of analysis, manifest in the discernment of fact from fiction, spurring informed dialogue necessary for resolution.

Through a tumultuous landscape carved by partisanship, our analytical foundations have served as an unshakeable core. As we have seen, bipartisan cooperation isn't just a lofty ideal; it's a feasible strategy when approached with a tactical mindset. Republicans and Democrats alike must use analytical thinking to critique and refine their strategies to better serve the nation. This sort of introspection catalyzes genuine progress.

Turning to the ideological battlefields, our book has dispelled the myths and realities of the socialist threat in America, steering the conversation back to the grounding principles of conservatism. At every juncture, analytical rigor punctuates our counter-narratives, laying bare the principles that have fortified our society for centuries and will continue to do so into the future.

The intersection of faith and freedom too demands our diligent analytical approach. By examining the historical and constitutional underpinnings of our nation, we reaffirm the balance of religious rights with secular governance, ensuring that every creed and conviction finds its place under the broad sky of American liberty.

America's right to bear arms is a testament to the import of historical context. An analytical reading of the Second Amendment — its roots, its evolution, and its present-day implications — fortifies public discourse, arming it with balanced perspectives that defend American freedoms against modern challenges. Such understanding is critical to the strengthening of any advocacy.

In facing economic warfare, America's capitalist spirit is not only under siege but often misunderstood or misrepresented. To defend our prosperity and drive for innovation, we must wield analysis to envision fiscal challenges through the eyes of our adversaries, ensuring that our defenses are as formidable as the entrepreneurial dreams they protect.

The omnipresent realm of cyber frontiers reveals a battleground where analysis intersects with anticipation. America's cyber strategies, strengthened through an understanding of potential threats, create bulwarks against digital hostility, securing our nation's valuable infrastructure and, more importantly, the trust of her people.

On the global chessboard, our nation's prowess emanates from a foundation of deep-seated analysis, leveraging insights into the psychology and tactics of global adversaries. This has empowered us to protect American interests and project our strength far beyond our borders, influencing the international narrative while safeguarding our homeland.

Our scrutiny does not shy away from the medical battlefield, where we navigate the treacherous waters of pandemic politics with precision. Scrutinizing political responses to public health crises reveals the chasms and triumphs, urging a calibrated response that places the well-being of citizens at the vanguard of policy-making.

Educational crossfire, an area where our youth and our collective future are shaped, benefits immensely from analytical insight. It is here that we recognize the value in preserving and teaching American history and ideals, ensuring our academic institutions are not just places of learning, but also guardians of national essence.

As we press forward, embracing the analytical vanguard is not an end but a starting point — a soaring launch pad for informed citizenship and enlightened governance. It beckons a future where challenges are met with a synthesis of insight, fortitude, and the sort of passionate clarity that has long been the hallmark of American spirit.

We find ourselves now armed with a more profound understanding and a steadfast commitment to the values that have steered this nation from its inception. The trials faced in the furnace of debate have only tempered our resolve, refining the American ethos that pulses through our culture and political endeavors.

To an engaged citizenry, the analytical vanguard is more than just an approach to national issues; it's a clarion call to be ever vigilant, ever thoughtful, and unwavering in the pursuit of truth. In embracing the analytical vanguard, we assure that our nation's dialogue remains rooted in the sound judgment and wisdom that are the bedrock of democracy's greatest champions. Let us steadfastly hold to this course, for in analysis lies the power to illuminate the path toward a more perfect union.

Appendix A

In the vein of thoughtful contemplation, we turn our gaze toward the underpinnings that have shaped our great nation. The soil of America's political landscape is rich with the philosophic efforts of our Founding Fathers, and it is upon us to study these carefully. In "Appendix A," we present a curated selection of the historical documents that serve as the stalwarts of American foundational thought. While we cannot encompass the full breadth of such integral works, what follows is a reflective embrace of extracts from these documents offering a lens through which to consider the current issues our nation faces.

The Federalist Papers, composed by advocates for the new Constitution, remain today a seminal guide for interpreting the intent behind the clauses of the Constitution. The correspondence between the builders of American governance unveils the intricacies of the law and its guardianship of liberty. Moreover, the Declaration of Independence proclaims the virtuous aspirations of a nascent republic yearning to breathe free from the dominion of empires prosaic and monolithic.

What's more, insights extracted from the histories written by early American observers provide a clear window into the onset of our national narrative, ripe with the fervor of revolution and the sapient foresight of an experimental democracy. The Charters of Freedom — The Declaration of Independence, The Constitution, and The Bill of Rights — are the real linchpins within these pages.

These founding documents are not mere words etched into antiquity; they are beacons that continue to navigate the path of a nation compelled to seek a 'more perfect union.' Their enduring relevance echoes the immutable spirit of the American ethos — a spirited commitment to freedom, justice, and unyielding resoluteness in the face of adversity.

Embedded within these texts is the heritage of analytical dispute and dialog that form the heart of American political discourse. As this grand examination of an analytical point of view on the complications of our nation unfolds, recognizing the prevailing ideals and principles that guided our country's inception is indispensable.

This compendium of formational documents draws a direct line from the revolutionaries' debates to the present-day discussions in town halls, legislative chambers, and everyday American homes. It is our hope that by immersing yourselves in these foundational pieces, you will gain a deeper understanding and equipped perspective to engage with the continual shaping of our nation.

As we navigate the challenges before us — held in the illumination of historical context — it is this cornerstone of our heritage that can inform a principled and proactive stance in the face of the evolving issues that test the fabric of our society. May we turn to these historical documents not as distant relics but as living instruments, both sword and shield, in the arenas of modern ideological battle and governance.

1. The Declaration of Independence

2. The Constitution of the United States

3. The Bill of Rights

4. Selections from The Federalist Papers

5. Notable Correspondence from American Founders

With reverence to our history and the inalienable rights enshrined therein, let the perusal of these documents reinvigorate your resolve to partake in the grand American journey. And it is in knowing where we come from that we can most effectively chart the course of where we must go. Together, let's renew our deference for the legacy that propels us forward as we continue to forge our national story.

A: Historical Documents of American Foundation

The bedrock of the United States lies in its historical documents, which not only illuminate the nation's origins but also speak to the enduring principles that guide its path forward. These documents, forged in the crucible of revolution and innovation, encapsulate the aspirations of a fledgling nation poised to define itself amidst the backdrop of an older world order.

The Declaration of Independence, proclaimed on July 4, 1776, is the resounding announcement of sovereignty that continues to reverberate across the annals of time. It posits that all men are created equal and are endowed with unalienable rights, among these life, liberty, and the pursuit of happiness. This revolutionary assertion set the stage for democratic governance and personal freedoms on a scale the world had yet to witness.

Woven into the fabric of the United States constitution is a masterful blueprint for government, a structural reinforcement balancing power and ensuring accountability. Ratified in 1788, it became the supreme law of the United States, outlining the branches of government and their respective powers, while safeguarding the individual liberties of its citizens.

The Federalist Papers, though not a formal legal document, serve as a comprehensive rationale for the newly drafted constitution, penned by founding luminaries like Hamilton, Madison, and Jay. It provides a deep dive into the thinking and philosophy that underpinned the American system, a reference point for scholars and patriots alike to understand the original intent of the nation's architects.

The Bill of Rights, the first ten amendments to the constitution ratified in 1791, reinforces and specifies the freedoms outlined in the original document, offering enhanced protections and liberties to people in the face of potential governmental overreach. These tenets support the right to free speech, protection against unreasonable searches, and the safeguarding of due process.

The Emancipation Proclamation of 1863 and the Gettysburg Address delivered in the same year by President Lincoln mark pivotal moments in the nation's history. They redefined the course of the Civil War, shifted the federal approach to the institution of slavery, and reaffirmed the principle that all men are created equal.

Antiquity bears witness to our nation's resolve through the Monroe Doctrine, a policy dictum of 1823 that shaped foreign policy, asserting American interest in the western hemisphere and serving notice to colonial European powers. This critical stance would not only shape U.S. foreign relations but also usher in a new era of American influence.

Subsequent documents, such as the women's suffrage amendment in 1920, complement these foundational materials by ensuring that the nation's evolution matches the enlightened ethos upon which it was conceived. It is an affirmation that the principles of liberty and justice adapt to an expanding understanding of human rights.

Thrown into sharp relief against this backdrop are lesser-known but equally significant writings like the Alien and Sedition Acts, which remind us of past struggles with balancing national security and free expression. They serve as an admonition against the overextension of state power, especially when fueled by fear and uncertainty.

The Louisiana Purchase treaty of 1803 and the Alaska Purchase of 1867 are not to be overlooked. As contracts, they may seem mundane, but as historical documents, they narrate a country's manifest destiny—an expansion from sea to shining sea that underscores American ambition and optimism.

Authorities like the Homestead Act of 1862 also capture a vision of boundless opportunity, promising public lands to settlers willing to cultivate and inhabit, thus fueling westward migration and contributing to the tapestry of the American Dream.

Each document, each declaration, exists not only as a historical record but also as a living testament to the American spirit. They map out the trajectory of a nation conceived in liberty and dedicated to the proposition of equality and justice for all.

The preservation of these artifacts is thus more than mere curation; it is a safeguard of the ideational lineage of the United States. It serves as both compass and touchstone for policymakers, legal scholars, and citizens, guiding and reminding them of the foundational pillars upon which the nation rests.

As we contemplate the myriad challenges that face contemporary society, we cannot divorce ourselves from the corpus of documents that have animated the American conscience since its inception. The examination of these documents transcends academic exercise; it is an ever-present call to ensure that the present and future of America aligns with the timeless tenets that are enshrined within these sacred texts.

In this perpetual endeavor, we recognize that these historical documents of American foundation are not merely the end of a conversation but the beginning of a dialogue—a dialogue that every American is a part of and contributes to, as guardians of a legacy that is ever-evolving and yet, unwavering in its core convictions.

Appendix B:
Glossary of Political and Strategic Terms

In the realm of political and strategic discourse, there's a litany of terms that shape our nation's discussions and decisions. The following definitions clarify essential language used to dissect the art of statecraft and to expound on the crucial ideas presented throughout this volume:

Adversary

An adversary in politics is an entity or group that opposes a particular stance, policy, or party. It's not limited to foreign actors; adversaries can be domestic, holding competing interests or ideological viewpoints.

Bipartisanship

Bipartisanship refers to the cooperation between two political parties that typically oppose each other's policies and stances. In the American context, it often involves Democrats and Republicans coming together to pass legislation that serves the broader interest despite their ideological differences.

Capitalism

A system of economics that is characterized by private ownership of resources and the means of production. Profits are generated through the operation of free markets where competition dictates success and failure.

Cyber Strategy

This pertains to a comprehensive approach in securing a nation's cyber infrastructure, which encompasses government networks, private sector assets, and the general public's connectivity. It entails defensive and offensive postures in the cyber realm to protect national interests.

Faith-Based Values

Values that stem from religious beliefs and serve as a moral compass for individuals and policymakers in society. They often intersect with political decisions, influencing issues from social policy to questions of rights and freedoms.

Immigration Policy

These policies define how a country manages and controls the flow of people across its borders: who may enter, how long they may stay, and under what conditions. It's a point of significant contention and political debate, particularly amid concerns of national security, economic impact, and cultural integration.

Intelligence and Counterintelligence

Intelligence refers to the gathering and analysis of information that is used to inform national security decisions. Counterintelligence involves activities aimed at protecting one's own classified information against espionage from foreign or domestic adversaries.

Marxism

A socio-political and economic ideology originating from Karl Marx's works, envisioning a society where the working class overthrows capitalist structures to achieve a classless society. The term is often used in contemporary political debates to critique various socialist-leaning policy proposals.

Partisanship

The unwavering support for a political party or stance, often leading to gridlock and the inability to reach a compromise. Analysis of partisanship is crucial for understanding the operational behaviors of political entities and their effects on policymaking.

Pathogen Politics

This is the intersection of public health issues, particularly epidemics and pandemics, with political action or inaction. It's crucial for understanding the way political agendas can influence, and sometimes polarize, public health responses.

Second Amendment Advocacy

The movement to protect the constitutional right to bear arms has various stakeholders, including individual citizens, interest groups, and policymakers. Advocacy efforts manifest in various forms, from litigation to public relations campaigns.

Socialist Threat

Generally refers to the perceived jeopardy to capitalist structures and principles from socialist ideology. This term also encapsulates debates over policies that are characterized as moving towards wealth redistribution, social welfare programs, or government control of resources.

Strategic Foresight

A discipline that prepares for possible future scenarios by understanding current trends and predicting their potential developments. In politics, it informs long-term planning and policy-making to navigate complex global dynamics.

Think Tank

An institution that performs research and advocacy in areas such as social policy, strategy, economy, military, technology, and culture. Findings from think tanks help shape public opinion and are often used to inform government policies.

Xenophobia

It is the fear or hatred of that which is perceived to be foreign or strange. Xenophobia can manifest in politics as policies that are hostile to immigrants and foreign entities. Understanding xenophobia is crucial for examining the underlying biases in nationalist ideologies and immigration debates.

These terms embody the profound issues at the heart of our nation's dialogues and conflicts, painting a complex picture of the strategies and ideologies at play. What emerges is a portrait of a country perpetually wrestling with its foundational tenets, each element a pixel in a larger political mosaic. As we navigate our political reality, may this glossary serve as a beacon, illuminating the pathways through which our nation might aspire to the ideals laid out in our foundational documents.

C: Further Reading and Resources

The pursuit of knowledge is an endless odyssey that is both exhilarating and vital, especially when it comes to the issues that shape our nation. Arming yourself with a diverse array of perspectives and deepening your understanding beyond the pages of this book plays a crucial role in refining the analytical mindset we aim to cultivate.

To venture further into the epochal debate of ideology and strategy, there is no better companion than a robust reading list that challenges and expands your horizons. The following recommended titles delineate various contours of the political, social, and economic landscape that our nation traverses, and they present arguments that range from time-honored philosophy to cutting-edge analysis.

Beginning with the philosophical underpinnings of the American political system and its adversaries, one must not neglect the seminal works of the founding fathers and political theorists. The "Federalist Papers" by Alexander Hamilton, James Madison, and John Jay provide rich insights into the architecture of American governance. Alexis de Tocqueville's "Democracy in America" is an indispensable study of American society and its democratic institutions.

For a more contemporary perspective, one should explore "The Righteous Mind: Why Good People are Divided by Politics and Religion" by Jonathan Haidt. It offers a profound understanding of the moral psychology that drives political factions and partisanship. Similarly, "The Clash of Civilizations and the Remaking of World Order" by Samuel P. Huntington probes into the global dynamics that influence American politics.

Engaging with the critical issues of national security and intelligence, "The Art of Intelligence: Lessons from a Life in the CIA's Clandestine Service" by Henry A. Crumpton provides a lucid account of the intelligence world. A complementary read would be "Playing to the Edge: American Intelligence in the Age of Terror" by Michael V. Hayden.

On the contentious topic of immigration, "The Death of the West: How Dying Populations and Immigrant Invasions Imperil Our Country and Civilization" by Patrick J. Buchanan offers a stark perspective that has sparked much debate. Delving into economic strategy, "The Price of Greatness: Alexander Hamilton, James Madison, and the Creation of American Oligarchy" by Jay Cost questions the economic ideals that have shaped American history.

Given the omnipresent challenge of cyber security, "The Art of Invisibility: The World's Most Famous Hacker Teaches You How to Be Safe in the Age of Big Brother and Big Data" by Kevin Mitnick is a compelling guide for understanding and navigating digital threats. "Lights Out: A Cyberattack, A Nation Unprepared, Surviving the Aftermath" by Ted Koppel also delves deep into the implications of a major cyber threat to national security.

On the international front, "The Chessboard and the Web: Strategies of Connection in a Networked World" by Anne-Marie Slaughter reinterprets global strategic frameworks in the context of interconnectedness. Graham Allison's "Destined for War: Can America and China Escape Thucydides's Trap?" explores the challenging dynamics between a rising power and a ruling one.

For those interested in the intersection of healthcare and politics, "The Politics of Fear: Médecins Sans Frontières and the West African Ebola Epidemic" edited by Michiel Hofman and Sokhieng Au is a vital resource that unpacks the global political response to health crises. "The Great Influenza: The Story of the Deadliest Pandemic in History" by John M. Barry takes a historical look at the political implications of pandemics.

Looking at education and culture, "The Closing of the American Mind" by Allan Bloom explores questions of higher education and cultural shifts. "Cultural Literacy: What Every American Needs to Know" by E.D. Hirsch, Jr., emphasizes the importance of shared knowledge for effective participation in civic life.

Moving forward, immersing oneself in these resources is an ongoing process that demands an agile mind and a passionate heart. Let the voices within these pages act as guides, challengers, and inspirers on your intellectual journey. Remember that learning is not a passive process—it involves active discussion, critique, and an intention to apply the knowledge gained towards problem-solving in the real world.

Alongside these readings, one should remain attentive to scholarly articles, journals, and respected publications that provide continuous examination and discourse on current events and policy debates. A commitment to continuous learning and analysis is at the core of maintaining an informed and proactive stance as citizens and advocates for a nation that holds true to its foundational promises of life, liberty, and the pursuit of happiness.

www.ingramcontent.com/pod-product-compliance
Lightning Source LLC
Chambersburg PA
CBHW072204280526
45788CB00002B/870